LUCCA

Town of art

Sole distributor
SANTORI S.A.S.
Via Busdraghi, 37 - Lucca

EDITION

officina
grafica
bolognese

HISTORY

Lucca owes its birth to the Ligurians, Etruscans and Romans, although previous discoveries witness human settlements dating back to the Palaeolithic Era. Its name is most probably due to the Ligurian Celts, who called the place "Luk", meaning "area of marshes".

Although the name dates back to that period (or so say the scholars), it was not until about the 3rd century bC that, thanks to the Romans, Lucca took on the aspect of an important centre, becoming a well-known Roman piazza (i.e. square).

A bit longer than a century later, around 180 bC, it became a Latin colony and in '89 a Roman municipality. It is important to remember that the famous encounter between Caesar, Crasso and Pompey took place here in 56 bC. But the most brilliant years occurred during the first two centuries of the Christian Era, of which there are some superlative evidences: a circle of walls, the Anfitheatre, etc. Its arrangement in a strategic position has quite encouraged life here: not only do many roads such as the Clodia, the Aurelia and the Cassia wind around Lucca, but both the Goths and the Longobards considered it (and declared it) to be the capital town of Tuscia. Having converted to Catholicism, the latter divided this area into Dioceses with different Parishes, therefore giving rise to another period of the town's politic and economic splendour. But it was not until the First Crusade (which Lucca's inhabitants widely took part in) that the town further enlarged its prestige becoming a Commune, and in the 13th century its fame started to expand so much that it became a large centre of commerce not only with Europe but also with the East (it became famous especially for its silk). And again it was in this period that the centre of Lucca was enriched with architectonic beauties (see the second circle of walls, many churches, etc.); even the houses were made to look more attractive and they started to be built in the shape of towers, often decorated with green tufts on the top. At the same time, though, internal and sanguinary fights started between the feudal aristocracy and the "merchant" middle-classes (the Ghibellinis and the Guelfis) and then, when the latter won, between the Bianchis and the Neris. In the end, it was the Neris who prevailed, forever banishing the Antelminellis from town. But Lucca owes Castruccio Castracani, one of the most famous representatives of this family, one of the most brilliant moments of its history.

The great leader, in fact, managed to extend the power of his town over great part of Tuscany. At his death, the town fights started again, therefore making Lucca a domain of its rival, Pisa.

Aerial view: in the foreground the Walls and the Cathedral of San Martino

From 1400 and for 30 years, Paolo Guinigi was Lord in Lucca; his power in those years is proved by numerous buildings, such as the Guinigi Palace, the homonymous villa and Jacopo della Quercia's sarcophagus in which lies Ilaria del Carretto, his young wife. At his fall, caused by Francesco Sforza's nobles, the republic of Lucca came across some difficult moments; the neighbouring Florence gained supremacy over the territory. So the entire concept of life in the town changed: now people were aiming at self-defence (a new circle of walls was built to try and stop enemy attacks) and concentrating no longer on commerce, but on agriculture. In this period, the 16th century, many beautiful countryside villas, of which we can still see the remains today, were built. With no great excitement, the republic of Lucca lived quietly until the end of the 18th century, when it was taken over by Napoleon's Empire. It was changed into a principality and assigned to Elisa Baciocchi, the Emperor's sister, until 1814; three years later it was annexed to the Granducato of Tuscany and then, together, they became part of the Italian Kingdom.

1: Aerial view of the whole circle of walls
2: View of bell-towers and towers
3: The city at dawn

THE TOWN

Lucca deserves to be seen and admired not only for the works of art it encloses, but also for being a rare and precious example of an almost intact historic centre. We shall therefore stop on this point before describing its monuments.

The urban structure is and has remained typically Roman-medieval. The *cardo maximus* and the *decumanus maximus*, the two main routes which divided the Roman *castrum* square hortogonally and met in the Forum (by the present Piazza San Michele, called "in Foro") are still clearly identifiable in the two main directrices represented by Via Cenami and Via Fillungo (north-south) and by Via San Paolino, Via Roma, Via Santa Croce (east-west). Rather evident, although more deformed and ruined, are even the minor routes (*cardines* and *decumani minores*) which run parallel to the former, dividing the urban surface into *insulae*.

Within these blocks, the accumulation of buildings in the Middle Ages has formed a complex interlacement of alleys, little winding roads and inner courtyards which are all connected to one another by vaults, passages and small irregular asymmetrical squares.

From an architectonic point of view, though, the substantial stability of the urban structure, does not mean that the town stopped a long time ago in history. On the contrary. Excluding the main churches, we can say that there are really very few buildings and environments that have not been more or less deeply readapted in the centuries. The town has never stopped renovating itself, adapting to the new needs and to the changes of general taste. But this happened not with radical distructions, but rather by means of a work of adaptation and modernization of old buildings, saving what could be re-used. Often in the asymmetry of plans and prospects or in the detail of certain solutions, the adaptation of a pre-existing situation is evident. So, the buildings from the 16th, 17th and 18th century are not isolated buildings in the town, but their presence does not upset the character and balance of the city. Even the changes in taste and style which mark the compositive and decorative elements of the façades, do not bring about ruptures or contrasts: tradition is never rejected, only constantly re-elaborated. This urbanistic, architectonic and stylistic continuity, which ran uninterrupted almost until the end of the 19th century, gave the town its precise and unique aspect. The (thank God, rare) monstrosities that hit us here and there, were built in recent times and really remain alienated from the surroundings.

Lucca was saved from the distructions which destroyed the most important Italian urban centres in the last century by the presence of the mighty city walls dating back to the 16th century. Because of their size (it would not have been easy to destroy them) and because they have always been loved by the citizens. The walls have resisted intact and they enclose and isolate the town in their green circle, so let's start our tour from them.

View from the Cathedral campanile

5

THE WALLS

There are many walled-in towns in Italy, but only a few, like Lucca, can boast as many as four circles of walls which are in great part still standing. The first circle was built by the Romans in a quadrangular shape, presumably 8-9 metres high; it used to run along the present Via della Rosa, Via dell'Angelo Custode, Via Mordini, Via degli Asili, Via San Giorgio, Via Galli Tassi, Via San Domenico, Via della Cittadella and Corso Garibaldi.

It was made of large blocks of limestone, but not much of it is left today, although there is still a section to be seen in the church of Santa Maria della Rosa.

There were four gates in these walls: one to the north, later called "San Frediano gate" which lead to the Clodia and to the Cassia towards Parma; one to the east, later called "San Gervasio gate", opening up onto the roads to Florence and Rome; one to the south, later called "San Pietro gate" leading to Pisa; and one to the west, renamed "San Donato gate", which led to Luni.

The second circle of walls is medieval and its construction went from the 12th to the 13th century. The town had by then spread out to north-east, and so it became necessary to protect the new areas (the San Frediano, the San Pietro Somaldi and the Santa Maria Forisportam districts).

The wall was built with square stones and had four gates, two of which are still standing: **the Borghi gate** and **the San Gervasio e Protasio gate.**

Like the other two, these gates had a drawbridge over the outer moat and also two side towers. A few years later, Castruccio Castracani committed Giotto to plan a further defence inside this circle of walls, called the Augusta, which covered about a quarter of the territory between two sides of the walls.

The third circle dates back to the 16th century.

It was made with large towers limiting a further part of territory on the north-east side, whereas large circular towers were built along the old fortifications to the south and west.

And finally the fourth circle, whose grandeur still leaves visitors speechless. Its building lasted over a century because of its incredible extension: 4200 metres.

But apart from its length we must not forget that along its "run" around town there were eleven bulwarks, twelve screens (with long rows of plants) and an external ditch with its embankment and "halfmoons".

A colossal work of art to which even private citizens contributed with tens of carts of stones.

Behind the "trunnions" of the bulwarks lay the artillery: 126 cannons which remained untouched until 1799, when the Austrians removed them. They were not only used for

2

3

1 : Bastion of Liberty
2: The Walls (16-17th cent.)
3: Santa Maria gate - Inside
4: Santa Maria gate - Exterior

4

defence but also as powder-magazine, as asylum and as place for provisions: in fact, the underground rooms with their stone vaults were used to stock munitions and as much as would be necessary to resist an attack.

Originally, there were three gates: **the San Donato**, **the San Pietro** and **the Santa Maria gate**. Napoleon's sister had the fourth gate, **Porta Elisa**, opened up onto the east side of the town in 1804. Two more, finally, **Porta San Jacopo** and **Porta Sant'Anna**, were opened in more recent times. The odd thing is that the great and majestic fortification was never really used to defend the town from enemy attacks; it became precious in 1812 when it saved Lucca from being swept away by a flood. In fact, the river Serchio overflowed and flooded the surrounding countryside, but the town managed to remain dry by simply closing its gates hermetically. A bizarre anecdote is that of when Elisa Bonaparte Baciocchi heard about the flood and tried to get back into town, but to do so she had to be levered over the walls by a crain.

The present disposition of the city walls is very much pleasing to the eye: parks, gardens and a "promenade" make them memorable.

1: S. Donato gate
2: Bulwark of San Paolino - Inside

THE CATHEDRAL

According to the tradition, the primitive church of San Martino was built by San Frediano in the 6th century. Bishop Anselm da Baggio, who then became Pope Alexander II, rebuilt it from the 5-nave foundation and solemnly consacrated it in 1070 in the presence of Matilde di Canossa. But not much is left of this building. The present aspect of the cathedral is the result of a long remake which started in the 12th century and finished in the second half of the 15th century, except for some minor later enlargements. The most ancient part is the façade. It was built on the edge of an existing portico and it leans onto the old anselmian façade by means of two arches over the entrance-hall vault. Above this was an air space which was then opened towards the inside. Around the middle of the 12th century the arches of the portico were already complete; the upper part came later: on the scroll ornament sustained by a male figure in the last cippus towards the bell-tower of the first little loggia there is an inscription stating that Guidetto da Como worked here in 1204. Between 1233 and 1257 the façade wall and the portal in the entrance-hall were decorated, whereas the apse - and the two head chapels of the naves and the north transept - were started in 1308, considerably enlargeing the pre-existing anselmian plan eastwards. In 1372, after having consulted some of the most important architects of the time (like Simone di Francesco Talenti), starting from the apse area which turned out to be dangerously instable, a general renovation of the inside was undertaken so as to restructure it in three naves. The adoption of the cross-vault instead of the truss cover meant changing monolithic columns for cross-shaped pilars as well as building counterforts on the sides.

Aerial view of the Cathedral

The works ended in the 15th century, outside, with the decoration of the central nave and, inside, with the creation of mullioned windows with three lights in the women's gallery. The two chapels on both sides of the apse belong to a later period: the one to the south, the Cappella del Sacramento (i.e. the Sacrament Chapel) was built in the first half of the 16th century by Vincenzo Civitali; the other one, the Cappella del Santuario (i.e. the Sanctuary Chapel) by Muzio Oddi da Urbino a century later. The long period of time in which it was being built and therefore the overlapping of taste through the years (as well as some very different hands and personalities working on it), though, have not produced great discord in the Cathedral. In spite of the great chronological inequalities, there has been a great sense of continuity between the parts and a spirit of harmonic adaptation which allowed this monumental work to turn out substantially homogeneous.

The Cathedral
1: Aerial view of the apse
2: The Façade

THE FAÇADE

The façade of San Martino has remained unfinished, that is to say, lacking the last row of small loggias and the tympanum.

What strikes most, though, is the remarkable asymmetry deriving from the fact that the right arch is much smaller than the other two.

As we said before, the façade is the only authentic Romanesque part and it is also the most original and significant.

Up to this moment, the Romanesque style in Lucca had been very much characterised by the linear purity of the architectonic whole, almost without decoration (see the church of Sant'Alessandro and the most ancient part of San Frediano). Here, in the façade of San Martino, for the first time we recognise the witness of remote and different artistic expressions which spread along the pilgrims' route, of which Lucca was one of the important stops.

The entrance-hall with its three mighty arches has no precedents in the architecture of the time. This work, which has great inventive power, clearly reveals the artist's Padanian formation. But in the complex sculptural decoration, especially in the third pillar from the left, beyond the Lombard artist, there are traces of an artist from the region of Apulia using Byzantine motives. The monumental precedent of the upper part is most certainly the Cathedral in Pisa. But although the architect Guidetto da Como reproposed the scheme of rows of superimposed small loggias, he really took his distance from it, therefore coming to a totally different result.

The geometric brightness of Rainaldo's Pisan façade (in which friezes, sculptures and inlays symmetrically stress the architectonic lines) here is out-of-date and upset by the gushing plasticity and colour energy of the Lombard masters.

The green and white inlay with different images - coats of arms, rosettes, zoomorphic or vegetal subjects which recall motives similar to those on the Lucchese silks from the same period - spreads freely over all the surfaces, while the sculptural decoration concentrates more on capi-

tals, on cornices and on corbels, filling them all with dragons, mermaids, lions, battles between men and wild beasts. The imagination of the Lombard masters is evident especially in the extreme diversification of the stems of columns: some are totally engraved, others in the shape of a spyral or gushing out of a dragon's mouth, others composed of four smaller knotted columns, the most simple ones decorated by chequered or herring-bone shaped inlays.

Of all the statues which must have sustained the corbels on different levels, the only one which has reached us belongs to the group of "Saint Martin and the Poorman", which is now inside the church and has been replaced on the façade by a moulding in cement.

For a long time, this unique work of art originated contrasts among critics, for some suggested it date back to the 12th century, others to the 14th and others still to the 15th century.

Today it is generally recognised as being a deed by a Byzantine artist living in the first half of the 13th century. The Romanesque architects obviously held in mind the existing bell-tower and so they solved this problem with their usual freedom and open-mindedness. It is interesting to notice how in the piazzas in Lucca the access streets are never in axis with the main building, which therefore appears to be in a corner. This was also the case of Piazza San Martino, whose buildings have now vanished: for those coming from north-west along the wall of the church of San Giovanni, the foreshortening effect considerably reduces the importance of asymmetry. One last important thing is that the façade of San Martino was raised compared to the original body, with a solution similar to the church of San Michele, built later by the same artists.

The Cathedral
1: Details
2: Façade on via del Battistero

THE ENTRANCE-HALL

The very rich decoration here does not spread like on the façade but it is strictly coordinated with the architectonic system made up of seven arches separated by jutting lions, in which there are also the three portals. The surfaces are divided in regular intervals by red and green marble stripes: in the checks there is a series of precious inlays, a Roman medallion (4th century) portraying an emperor, a Renaissance medallion representing the profile of the humanist Pietro d'Avenza, and on each side of the left door, two tombstones and a 13th century transcription of the old façade: the first, in hexametres, celebrates the rebuilding of the church by Pope Alexander II; the other, dating 1111, reports the honesty oath taken by money-changers whose counter was in the entrance-hall. On symmetrical panels higher up were the "Storie di San Martino (i.e. Saint Martin's Stories)" and the images of the Months.

It is impossible to identify the exceptional artist who worked here. Among the names provided by documents we can find Maestro Lombardo (probably Guidetto da Como's son) and Guido Bigarelli. It is believed that the latter - whose works are also to be found in Pisa and in Pistoia - may be the author of the general architectonic drawing, the decoration of the portals, the lintel of the main door "Maria degli Apostoli" (Mary of the Apostles) and the symbols of the Evangelists (the Eagle and the Angel). Maestro Lombardo is said to have created the lintel of the right door ("San Regolo disputa con i Goti ariani (i.e. Saint Regolo argues with the Arian Goths)") and, in the lunette, the beautiful "Martirio di San Regolo (i.e. Martyrdom of Saint Regolo)"; the lunette of the central

1: Entrance-hall - Main Portal and Right Portal
2: Central portal: lunette showing Christ rising to
  Heaven between two angels; on the lintel,
  the Apostles and Mary attending the Ascension
3: Atrium - Stories of St. Martin

13

door (Christ ascending between two Angels); the reliefs of "Storie di San Martino" on both sides of the main door; and below these, the images of the Months, with the Signs of the Zodiac in the imposts of the small arches. The high quality sculptures are characterised by balance of composition, solidity of structure and plastic energy.

Even Nicola Pisano's work is to be noticed in the entrance-hall: he planned the lintel of the left door (Annunciation, Nativity and Adoration of the Kings) and the splendid "Deposizione (i.e. Deposition)" in the lunette. This is considered to be the artist's first known work when he arrived to Tuscany from Apulia.

Above the minor arch looking towards Piazza Antelminelli there are the head of a figure with a mitre, inside, and, outside, a female bust: according to tradition they represent Pope Alexander II and countess Matilde. On the right half-pillar leaning against the bell-tower is the engraving of a symbolic Labyrinth which can also be found in other Italian churches of the time.

The Cathedral - Atrium
1: Stories of St. Martin
2-3: Symbols of the months
4: The Labyrinth
5: San Martino and the beggar (13th century)

THE INTERIOR

As we said before, the interior was completely rebuilt between 1372 and the end of the following century. The Gothic style was never much felt in Lucca where they tried to make the best of the new trends and the strong, still prevailing Romanesque building tradition. Although this is the only church in Lucca from that time to have vaults (the others, even the big ones, have trusses), even in San Martino the thin cross-shaped pillars and the vertical nave are very much minimised by the use of a round arch. The later phase of international Gothic is the time for elegant pointed-arched mullioned windows with three lights starting in the women's gallery and continuing even in the wall above the pillars dividing the transept. Although this is a bit of a stylistic compromise, it turns out to be very stimolating and impressive.

The church of San Martino is full of works of art, the most important of which we will talk about now. Entering the main door, on the right against the wall, we find the marble group of "San Martino e il povero", which used to be on the above mentioned façade. The Holy-water fonts by the first two pillars, as well as the creation of the floor, are by Matteo Civitali (1498). The floor is chequered in white and green marble and at the centre of each check there are coloured geometric inlays; it responds perfectly to the church's architectonic proportions. Walking down the right aisle, at the third altar, there is a "Last Supper" painted on commission by Tintoretto around 1590. Although the canvas was accomplished by different hands, it is remarkable for its dramatic perspective and conception of the light.

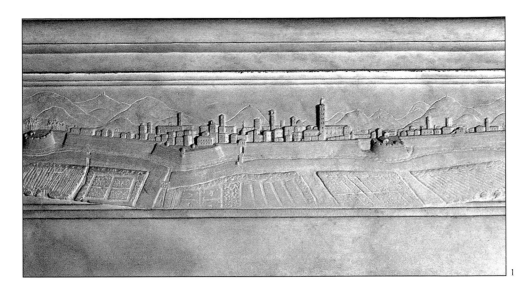

The Cathedral - Inside
1: Socle of the altar of liberty showing Lucca in the 16th cent. and the construction of the new city wall (1577). Low relief by John of Bologna
2: Detail of the arches between the aisles

A bit further on is the entrance to the vestry, rebuilt at the end of the 14th century and finished in 1404. The beautiful capitals of the semi-pillars witness the work of Jacopo della Quercia who was very active in the works of the Cathedral in those years. The famous sarcophagus of Ilaria del Carretto, Paolo Guinigi's second wife who died in 1405, has temporarily been placed inside. For its composition, this work by Jacopo della Quercia (1407-1408) recalls similar French monuments, but the Gothic taste here has been exceeded by a sensitivity which is typical of Renaissance. In spite of its great stylization, Ilaria is very much alive and leaves an unforgettable image in the soul of the spectator.

The typically classical puttos holding festoons on either side of the sarcophagus underline the calm and serene beauty of the young woman lying there. On one of the shorter sides is the coat of arms of the Guinigi-Del Carretto family. The bas-relief on the altar of Sant'Agnello, with the picture of the saint, is by Antonio Pardini da Petrasanta: a remarkable artist who has recently been rediscovered and revalued.

At this point we must talk about the outer decoration of the upper part of the apse, the transept and the nave which were long worked upon by many artists among which Antonio Pardini (directing the works between 1395 and 1419) and Jacopo della Quercia: these sculptures, especially the human heads on the arches' imposts, have acquired exceptional importance.

The Cathedral
1: Right Aisle: The Last Supper (Tintoretto 1590)
2-3: Detail of Ilaria del Carretto's Sarcophagus
(Jacopo della Quercia 1407-1408)

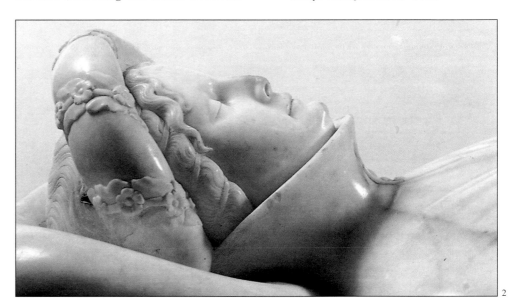

The picture called "Madonna on Throne among four Saints" on the altar of Sant'Agnello is by Domenico Ghirlandaio (1449-1494). His pupil Bartolomeo di Giovanni created the free and full-of-imagination scenes on the foot-pace. The completion lunette "Dead Christ sustained by Nichodemus on the Sepulchre" has been attributed to Filippo Lippi. In the vestry we can also see a picture of San Girolamo (some claim it was painted by Guercino and others by Paolo Biancucci), as well as another picture from the 15th century representing the "Nativity" and a 16th century picture by Jacopo Ligozi (also see the 1506 "Visit of Mary to Saint Elisabeth" by the same artist on the altar behind the small temple of the Holy Face). After the vestry we come to the right transept where there are various works by the Local artist Matteo Civitali, a great sculptor who has been unfairly disregarded by the critic, probably because he worked in a peripherical environment, yet participating in the figurative culture of his time.

Pietro da Noceto's sepulchral monument on the west wall is his first documented work (1472 - the artist was 36 years old) and it is also one of the most beautiful: Antonio Rossellino estimated it 450 gold ducats.

On the south wall is the austere funeral monument of the patron Domenico Bertini dating from 1479

4

5

19

In the years just before then, Matteo sculptured the two beautiful Adoring Angels in the nearby Sacrament Chapel: they were part of an altar which was unfortunately dismembered (the ciborium can probably be identified with the one in the Victoria and Albert Museum in London). Finally, at the top of the nave is the great altar-frontal of San Regolo (1484).

On the main altar is a 14th century triptych on a gold background: "Madonna fra Angeli e Santi (i.e. Madonna among Angels and Saints)" which used to be in the vestry.

After having crossed the presbytery we come to the left aisle at the top of which we find the altar of Liberty created by Giambologna in the years 1577-1579.

The beautiful and well-known central statue of the resuscitated Christ is for sure a deed of this Flemish artist, whereas the side statues of the Protector-Saints Peter and Paolino were made by his assistants.

In the foot-pace there is a beautiful 16th century bas-relief of a view of Lucca with its new circle of walls. The altar was ordered by the citizens to celebrate the freedom gained and then constantly kept from 1369.

In the nearby Sanctuary Chapel is the beautiful altar-piece by Frà Bartolomeo della Porta representing the Madonna with Her Child between two Saints, with two Angels holding a crown and a third one playing the lute at the foot of the throne.

The warm tones of the colours used in this painting, signed and dated 1509, reveal the Venetian influence in the formation of the Florentine painter. Many preparatory drawings of this work are to be found in the Uffizi Gallery, at the Louvre, in Chantilly and in Weimar.

The Cathedral - Sacristy
1: *Saint Matthew, Saint Peter led by the angel from his prison*
2: *Saint Clement thrown into the sea on Trajan's orders*
3: *Martyrdom of Saint Sebastian*
4: *Saint Paul's conversion, Saint Laurence*
5: *Presentation of Mary to the Temple (Alessandro Allori called Il Bronzino - 1598)*

20

FLORENTINVS CRISTOFERT DEPINGE...

THE HOLY FACE

Half way down the left aisle is the small octagonal temple, an elegant work by Matteo Civitali (1484) containing the famous wooden Crucifix known as "The Holy Face" or even "Santa Croce" (i.e. the Holy Cross).

According to the ancient legend, the Crucifix was carved into a cedar of Lebanon by Nicodemo, but the hand of the artist modelling the features of Christ was led by the Angels.

For centuries it was kept hidden because of the persecutions and then it was put on a boat and sent out to sea. Sailing miraculously through the Mediterranean and avoiding pirates, it managed to reach the beach of Luni. To entrust the choice of the seat to the divine will, the Holy Cross was put on a cart pulled by indomitable steer, which headed towards Lucca.

The transfer is said to have happened at the time of Bishop John I (8th century). The legend continues with the story of the Holy Face's first marvels, among which it is necessary to remember the one of the poor minstrel, the pilgrim Venuto di Francia. Feeling sorry for not being able to afford even a small offering, he expressed his devotion as well as he could: he played the lute in front of the sacred image. Jesus felt sorry for him and gave him one of his silver tiles, dropping it in front of him. Shortly after the minstrel was caught and con-

demned for sacrilegious theft, but he was recognised innocent and saved by Holy Intervention. Since then, one of the tiles of the Holy Face is sustained by a silver chalice. In the Middle Ages, the legend of the Holy Cross and the fame of its miracles followed the merchants from Lucca and spread very rapidly through all the countries, especially France, Flanders and London. The English King William II used to swear "per sanctum Vultum de Luca".

Great part of the propaganda for this legend was made by the minstrels, especially the French ones, who followed the pilgrimages all over Europe. Among the people in remote areas of the country who listened to the minstrels' songs, the cult of the Holy Face originated bizarre derivations. In some areas of France, for example, the people started venerating an unknown "Saint Vaudeluc" who was really only a misinterpretation of "Saint Vault de Lucques". Even the cult of the bearded crucified virgin, Saint Kummernis, in Germanic countries started more or less like that. The Holy Face soon became the symbol of Lucca: its image is to be found on the town's coins and on the seal of the Corte dei Mercanti; it is also quoted in Dante's 21st Canto of the Inferno. In the last century, the date of the Holy Face originated serious controversy and differences of opinion between critics and historians, also because tradition, documents - often difficult to value - and the stylistic features of the work seem to contradict one another. The prevailing opinion today is that the great Crucifix is the deed of a Lombard maestro from the second half of the 11th century (exactly the period in which Pope Alexander II promoted the renovation of the church in Lucca).

But on the other hand, from some documents it seems almost certain that the present Holy Face was preceded in San Martino by another crucifix, of which not much is known, except that it is much older: this could conciliate the tradition with the critic's opinion. Originally, the Holy Face was in polychromatic wood, but the blackening due to centuries of candle smoke and incense has provoked a very dark coating on the picture. This work is very severe but extremely beautiful. During the "Santa Croce" celebrations in September, the Holy Face is decorated with precious ornaments: a richly decorated tunic made of gold-embroidered velvet (14th century) and a gold crown and collar with a big jewel (17th century). Every year, on the 13th of September, at nightfall, a procession takes place through the town in memory of the transfer of the Holy Face.

The whole town takes part in this procession and the representatives of all the ancient dominions of the Republic carry a votive candle. Opposite the Chapel of the Holy Face is the "Presentation of Mary to the temple" by Alessandro Allori called il Bronzino, signed and

1

dated 1598. At the end of the aisle, on the inner wall of the façade, we see a fresco by Cosimo Rosselli, narrating some episodes from the legend of the Holy Face (about 1482). The church of San Martino has always been very rich in precious ornaments, as witnessed by inventories reaching us from 1239.

Unfortunately, numerous plunderages in the centuries have seriously depaupered this wealth: for example, the one in 1440 when all the churches in Lucca offered most of their silver to contribute to the defence of the town from the Florentines. It is necessary to remember the "The Pisans' Cross" both for its importance and for its fame among the citizens in Lucca.

It is called like this because, according to the legend, it was taken from the citizens of Pisa by fraud. Kept in the Museum of the Cathedral, it is 76 cm. tall, rests on an elonged hexagonal base, finely chiselled with flowers; on the recto there is a very rich pattern of leaves sustaining small statues (the Crucifix and the Eternal at the top; S.Marco and S.Luca at the ends of the oblique arm in two small tabernacles; San Matteo and two sorrowful figures at the bottom).

On the verso the cross is made of 24 lilies with a small figure of a prophet in each calyx.

This very high quality deed is considered to have been made by an ultramontane goldsmith at the end of the 14th century. As a rule, it is exposed on the main altar on the day of Santa Croce.

The Cathedral
1: Temple of the Holy Face (Matteo Civitali - 1484)
2-3-4: The Holy Face

On pages 24-25
The city seen from the Cathedral

23

THE MUSEUM OF THE CATHEDRAL

Opposite the left transept of the church of San Martino there lies the entrance to the Museum of the Cathedral, recently built to contain the early-Medieval ornaments for the celebration of solemn religious services in the Cathedral as well as the paintings and sculptures which lay partly in deposits and partly in the Cathedral's vestry (they were removed from their original position to be preserved, or replaced to satisfy the periodic changes in taste); as a consequence, they are not accessible to the public.

The dislocation of the works inside the building containing the Museum follows a chronological order to allow visitors to have a global perception of the artistic taste of each period; this is true everywhere, except for the hall containing all the miniature codes and anthembooks integrating the knowledge of painting in Lucca from the Middle Ages to the 15th century, all collected in one hall so as to allow the comparison of the sources of illumination. Among the exposed pieces, the most precious and rare are Areobindo's ivory diptych (6th century), the copper and enamel shrine from Limoges (representing the martyrdom of Thomas Becket and the ascent of his soul to Heaven), the famous flowered "Croce dei Pisani" and the painted leather shrine of Flemish make. The prosperous season of the figurative culture in Lucca (between the 15th and 16th century) is illustrated by Vincenzo Frediani's paintings, by Matteo Civitali's choral enclosure and by two silver works by Francesco Marti: the reliquary in the shape of a small circular temple and the pastoral with an image in its curl of Saint Martin giving the poorman his cloak.

The exposition of vestments and silk chasubles, sometimes embroidered with flowers and geometric patterns, certifies the high quality level reached and maintained by the textile manufacture in Lucca until the late 18th century. Furthermore, the Museum contains a considerable amount of silverware produced in Lucca between the 15th and the 19th century, most of which bearing hall-marks. The hall devoted to sculpture overlooks the Cathedral, allowing an immediate recall of the original setting of the exposed works: among these are the 11th century bishop's head (one of the rare examples of the Cathedral consacrated in 1070 by Anselmo da Baggio, bishop of Lucca and later Pope Alexander II) and the Apostle by Jacopo della Quercia, from one of the buttresses on the south side, symbolizing all those people who contributed to the expenses for the building of the Cathedral.

The tour around the Museum also includes a visit to the oratory of San Giuseppe (the ruins of the 16th century convent of the Gesuate nuns) enriched in the 17th century by paintings as well as by an inlaid and golded work in wood. The tour ends in the hall devoted to the ornaments for the Holy Face which are still used today on the 3rd of May and on the 14th of September to "dress" Christ's holy image kept in Matteo Civitali's small temple in the Cathedral. The same room contains the four statues of the Evangelists by the Fancellis (disciples of Bernini's), which in the past were located in the arches outside the temple of the Holy Face.

Among the most significant proofs of the devotion of Lucca's citizens to the sacred image, there are the 14th century ornament on Christ's gown, the luxurious golden crown with set jewels, the collar with an exuberant decoration produced around the middle of the 17th century, and the jewel surrounded by enamels and diamonds, referable to the French jeweller Gilles Légaré

who worked at the court of the Sun King. Outside the museum, along the north side of San Martino, we come to the back lawn, which is limited by the city walls on one side and on the other side by the Palazzo Arcivescovile (i.e. the Archbishop's Palace). From here, there is a most beautiful view of the whole back part of the church and of the bell-tower. Next to the palace are the Archbishop's Archives with their 15th century portal (Jacopo della Quercia's school). Herein are diplomas of emperors, papal bulls and more than 1,500 parchment papers from the 8th, 9th and 10th century, which are very important in the study of the Longobard and Carolingian period.

1: The building that houses the museum
2: Annunciation (Leonardo Grazia, early 16th century)
3: Frà Fazio (Anonymity - end of the 14th century)
4: The Holy Conversation (Vincenzo Frediani - end of the 15th century)

3

4

PIAZZA
S. MARTINO

The two piazzas (Piazza San Martino and Piazza Antelminelli connected to the nearby Piazza San Giovanni by a small stretch) on which the Cathedral rises, are among the most harmonious and stimulating places in town. The balance of the complex structure converges in the buildings overlooking it, yet being typical of very differ-

ent periods and styles. An admirable example of environmental respect and perfect urban positioning is represented by Palazzo Micheletti, ordered in the second half of the 16th century by Giovan Battista Bernardi, bishop of Ajaccio, the son of a very good merchant family in Lucca.

The excellent use of the ashlar-work which elegantly marks doors, windows, lintels and corners, is for sure a deed of Bartolomeo Ammannati, who in those years was in Lucca for the works on the Palazzo Pubblico.

Next to the transept of San Giovanni is a delightful small palazzo stretching into a high balustrade wall with two big windows on each side of the portal; the beautiful wall (and the garden it encloses) joins the two squares. One of the masters of this way of

working on - and yet not upsetting the existing architectonic environment is Lorenzo Nottolini, who in 1832 built the circular basin in Piazza Antelminelli. Although it is very much ruined and badly restored, the Casa dell'Opera del Duomo (i.e. the Cathedral Society) next to the church, is an important example of local 13th century building: its main features are the stone arches on the ground floor, which were originally open, the large mullioned windows with three lights on the upper levels and the polychromy of the materials used.

1: Casa dell'Opera del Duomo
2: Palazzo Micheletti

CHURCH OF S. GIOVANNI E S. REPARATA

Walking along the side of the church of San Giovanni, we come to the small square bearing the same name, which is also very harmonious and bright, although it lacks particularly interesting buildings. This church devoted to San Giovanni and Santa Reparata was Lucca's first cathedral until the 8th century.

Recent systematic excavations during works of consolidation have brought out the original floor with the base of the pillars and the crypt (5th and 6th century).

In the 12th century it was rebuilt from its foundations in the actual form: inside, in the three aisles, different shafts and some capitals from the imperial age were used, adapting them to different size bases.

1: The façade
2: The inside
3: The magnificent decorations of the entrance hall and architrave

The façade, which was remade in the early 17th century, still bears the Romanesque portal and a typically Lombard engraved lintel. Next to the church is the Battistero (i.e. Baptistery), rebuilt with a square plan in the 14th century and finished with an ogival dome in 1393. Excavations in the last century have brought out an ancient lustral basin, probably from the early Middle Ages, as well as fragments of a Roman black and white chequered floor, three metres under the present level.

1: The Baptistery dome
2: The Baptisimal font

GIGLIO THEATRE

From piazza San Giovanni we go to Piazza del Giglio, where we see the homonymous Neoclassical theatre by Lazzarini.

There is also an important monument to Garibaldi and two beautiful buildings: the **Paoli**, which is now a hotel, and the **Arnolfi palace**.

The Giglio theatre was very well-known at the beginning of the 19th century, when competing with the San Carlo theatre in Naples and also with the Scala in Milan for the privilege of presenting the latest shows.

1: The Giglio Theatre
2: The inside

DUCAL PALACE

It will seem natural to walk to the left from the Piazza del Giglio towards Piazza Grande and its most beautiful **Palazzo Ducale** (i.e. Ducal Palace), also called Palazzo della Signoria (at the times of the Republic) or simply Palazzo Pubblico, now office of the Province.

Its story is quite tormented because it rose on part of the area occupied by the Augusta fortress (which we spoke about in the chapter regarding the walls) and was commissioned by Castruccio Castracani in 1322.

At his death, though, the foreign rulers took over and this made the citizens identify the building with a symbol of slavery; so, as soon as they could, the people demolished it and left only the Palazzo Signorile. The Elders of the Republic settled there, abandoning their earlier seat in piazza San Michele.

This is where the Main Council met and even where the Gonfalonier lived; it is also the headquarter of the arsenal (also called Tersenaia), of the "Ministry of Finances" of the time (called "the Office above the entrance") with its Main Toll (the custom-house which collected considerable revenues for the State), and of the secret archive (called Tarpea).

Let's try and recollect the complex history of this building.

We know that in the middle of the 16th century there were three very different buildings in the southern part of the town.

The disastrous explosion of the powder-magazine in the tower of the palace, provoked by lightning in August 1576, caused serious damage to the entire building. Instead of restoring it, the inhabitants of Lucca decided to build a new seat for their government and so they assigned the project to Bartolomeo Ammannati who decided to supply it with a little wooden model, so as to emphasise the harmony of his work.

It took a long time to decide about the building, but then eventually it started, although already then the grandeur of the work appeared excessive for a town with no real great political activity.

Ammannati started following the construction of his work; the left part of the façade, the north wing on the "Cortile degli Svizzeri (i.e. Courtyard of the Swiss)" (where the guards working for the Republic lived) as well as the loggia, up to the main portal, are part of the original project. The former, with three openings spaced by windows, is decorated by a beautiful lacunar ceiling and a brick-work floor; ashlar work is to be found on the front door, on the pillars of the porch on the north and east sides of the Cortile degli Svizzeri.

The passageway of the front portal most probably was meant to be the base of the palazzo's tower, but for financial reasons it was never built. But this is not the only work to have been suspended: since it was necessary to fortify the town, Ammannati was dismissed and the building was left incomplete.

The building was not touched until the beginning of the 18th century. The job was handed on to Juvarra who presented two projects: the first, probably too ambitious and expensive, was put aside; the second, presented twenty years later, was accepted and started shortly after.

The façade

So the façade was completed, the north wing with the monumental entrance was built, and the second courtyard was restored because it had been severely damaged.

It was destiny that not even Juvarra could finish the work, so again the palace remained without its west side. The third "wave" of works came at the time of Elisa Bonaparte (with the building of the piazza named after her brother, obtained by demolishing many buildings) and of Maria Luisa di Borbone. It was she who gave the architect Lorenzo Nottolini the task to continue the works. The Passaggio delle Carrozze (i.e. the Passageway for the Coaches) was built to connect the two courtyards. The big 16th century staircase was also demolished and replaced by the "Scala Regia (i.e. the Royal Staircase)" ending in the "Galleria delle Statue (i.e. Statue Gallery)". The upper floor, too, was changed and divided into three parts. The first was made up of the "Quartiere di parata (i.e. Parade Quarter)" (with antechamber, meeting rooms and the King's private cabinet); the remaining two were made up of the King's and Queen's apartments. Obviously, the frescos, stuccos and bas-reliefs, as well as the furniture, were very luxurious. All those lovely things, though, have been lost, because when Lucca was annexed to the Italian Kingdom together with Tuscany, the palace and its contents became property of the Crown and ended up in the many royal houses throughout Italy. Therefore, in this tour it will be possible to admire only what could not be displaced, such as the splendid Scala Regia, the Galleria delle Statue, the Loggia, the Cortile degli Svizzeri and not much else. After having visited this splendid building, walking out of the Cortile degli Svizzeri, the tour around Lucca continues towards the church of San Romano, consecrated in 1281.

1: Courtyard of the Swiss
2: Statue's gallery

33

CHURCH OF SAN ROMANO

In the shape of a Latin cross and with only one nave and large windows, this church was built in stone in the second half of the 13th century.

In 1373, using bricks from the demolition of the Augusta fortress, the building was raised and enlarged in the area of the apse, adding on five chapels. Inside it was completely transformed in 1661 according to the taste of the time. A fly-over joined the church of San Romano to the nearby Palazzo Pubblico. The Dominicans, who were very important in the cultural and religious life of the Republic, lived in the annexed convent from 1281. On what used to be the east side of the cloister we can now see two mullioned windows with three lights and the door to the Aula Capitolare (i.e. Capitular Hall), which are all in a very bad state. Waiting to be placed somewhere else, here we find many 14th and 15th century relief tombstones taken from the floor of the church; among them are those of the seven Teutonic knights (who were constables of the Augusta) and that of Capoana Donoratico (the wife of the famous Conte Ugolino quoted by Dante).

Walking away from Piazza San Romano, we walk along Via Burlamacchi, and after crossing over Via Vittorio Emanuele, we enter Piazza Sant'Alessandro on the right.

The church of San Romano

34

CHURCH OF SAN ALESSANDRO

Built around the middle of the 11th century, Sant'Alessandro is the only church in Lucca from this time not to have undergone substantial transformation and remanagement: the only elements from a later period are the decoration of the completion of the apse, the typically Lombard hanging little arches (12th century) and the 15th century tabernacle placed over the side portal. This building is very interesting also because it is the most complete and perfect example of the early Romanesque style in Lucca, which was very different and independent from the Lombard and Pisan currents.

The church is almost completely without decorations, but its beauty is due to the pure and essential architectonic elements: the white hangings bordered in light grey, the very simple decoration around the small windows, the classic portal.

The upper part of the façade seems manhandled: the bases of the four columns on the horizontal cornice with lintelled loggia are similar to the façade of San Frediano, also from that period.

The same spirit reveals the interior which is also harmoniously bare and simple.

The colonnades are interrupted by two couples of pillars, originally limiting the choir enclosure. The only linear decorative elements are the cornices on the wall of the central aisle, one of which stops at the beginning of the presbytery. The Romanesque capitals are exceptionally beautiful. Most of the columns and capitals derive from Roman buildings.

Back on Via Burlamacchi, up to the cross-roads with Via San Paolino, then to the left, after a few steps, here we are in front of the beautiful and clear façade of the church of San Paolino.

1: Niche of the lateral portal (15th cent.)
2: The façade

35

CHURCH OF SAN PAOLINO

Dating from the first half of the 16th century, it was built by Baccio da Montelupo and entitled to Lucca's first bishop. It is built on a Latin cross plan (the aisles are not very deep) and it contains numerous paintings and wooden statues, as well as frescos narrating the legend of San Paolino, by the Certosino and by Filippo Gherardi, a 17th century artist from Lucca. The first altar, the one to the right, is devoted to the Trinity and was made by Riccio; the second one contains the "Madonna con Bambino e Santi (i.e. Madonna with Child and Saints)" by Ardenti; the third was made by Francesco Valdambrino in the 15th century; the fourth recounts the miracle of Saint Theodore and was made by Testa. Beyound the transept, there is a 14th century wooden Crucifix and on the side a "Seppellimento di San Paolino (i.e. Burial of San Paolino)" by Paolo di Lazzarino da Lucca. Another precious work in wood is the Angel, which is kept in a niche and dates back to the 14th century. The main altar was created in the 16th century. Behind it is a Paleochristian sarcophagus. On the left, in a niche, a work on wood by Certosino representing the Saint; in the chapel on the left an "Incoronazione di Maria (i.e. Coronation of Mary)" and opposite a "Madonna with Child and Saints", the former from the 15th and the latter from the 16th century. The first altar is enriched by a "Decapitazione di Valerio (i.e. Decapitation of Valerio)" by Guidotti, and the second altar by a German terracotta of a Madonna and Child. In the fourth altar there is a "Pietà" by Lombardi and in the vestry some works by Zacchia. Along the road, at a depth of three metres, the Roman paving of the decumano was found. After the church, we turn to the right down Via Galli Tassi where we see Palazzo Mansi, called "a San Pellegrino" because of the church it has in front.

1: The façade
2: Maria's Coronation between angels and saint, below a view of Lucca in the Middle Ages; Florentine school of the second half of the 15th c.

PALAZZO MANSI

This palace, built at the end of the 16th or at the beginning of the 17th century, has a deep entrance-hall looking onto the courtyard. The ground floor is occupied by halls devoted to public activities, whereas the floor at the top of the beautiful staircase is full of richly decorated rooms with 17th and 18th century furniture, sitting-rooms with tapestries from Brussels and the astonishing room called "degli sposi (i.e. the bride's and bridegroom's room)", enclosed in a golden Baroque cornice represented by the arch separating it from the rest of the hall. It is undescribable for the richness of its decorations (silks, stuccos, encarved wood) and for the excellent state it is kept in. Recently, the palace has passed in the hands of the State. In the rooms which used to contain the important Mansi picture-gallery (now lost) today we can see the Pinacoteca Nazionale (i.e. the National Picture Gallery). Most of it was founded thanks to the bountiful donation of the Grand Duke Leopoldo II of Tuscany in 1847 to the town as soon as it was annexed to his state, in return for the alienations and removals perpetrated by Carlo Ludovico di Borbone.

1: Crucifix figuring Saint Catherine of Alexandria and Saint Julius by Guido Reni (15th cent.)
2: Brussels tapestries realized after a drawing by Justus Egmont (1665)

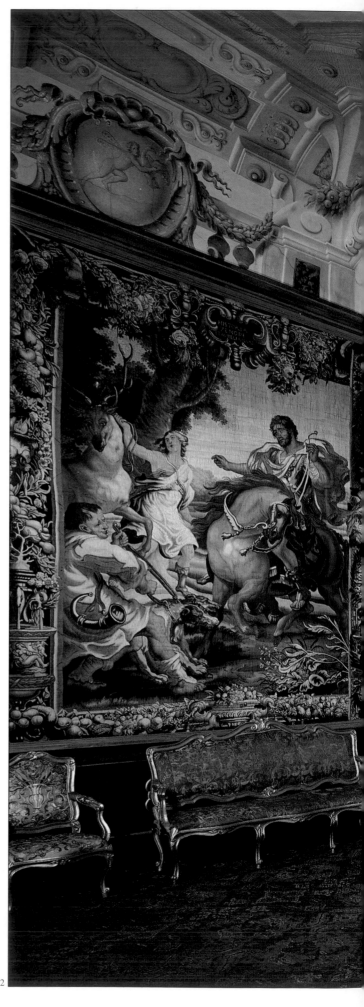

The pictures of the donation, made executive in 1861, come from the Guardaroba Mediceo (i.e. the Medici family wardrobe) and belong to the 16th and 17th century. Among the many precious pictures you may also see in the catalogue, the "Ritratto di giovinetto" (i.e. Portrait of a boy) by Pontormo (about 1525) and the picture of "La Continenza di Scipione" (which originally was the mirror over a wedding chest) painted by Domenico Beccafumi in the first years of the 16th century, are worthy of notice. Out of the Mansi Palace, down Via San Paolino, we come to Piazza Cittadella where the monument to the composer Giacomo Puccini has been placed (his house lies in the neighbouring Via di Poggio). At the end of this road we can see the façade of the church of San Michele.

Palazzo Mansi
1-2: Bride's and Bridegroom's Room
3: Scipio's abstinence (16th cent.) by the Sienese Domenico Beccafumi
4: Portrait of Giacomo Puccini by Edoardo Gelli
5: Portrait of a Boy (Pontormo - 1525 circa)

ST. MICHAEL CHURCH AND SQUARE

Placed on the area of the ancient Roman forum, this beautiful square has remained the centre of town in the centuries. Ulisse Cambi's monument to Francesco Burlamacchi was placed here in the last century, whereas in the 18th century it was repaved, limiting the spaces with small columns and chains. Before entering the church, take a look at the wrought iron lantern from the beginning of the 16th century and the Palazzo Pretorio (formerly "del Podestà") built at the end of the 15th century with its elegant loggia built in two different moments: in 1492 apparently on a project by Matteo Civitali (and according to somebody

1: The square seen from above
2: Palazzo Pretorio
3: St. Michael during the "Luminara"

On pages 44-45
1: Detail of the Façade
2: Matteo Civitali, The Virgin and Child
   (15th century)
3: Church and Campanile

3

by his son Nicolao) and in 1589 by *Vincenzo Civitale*.

Also the "palazzo del Decanato" is interesting: it is united to the church's transept by a sort of overpass attributed to Francesco Marti who built it in the year 1500 on the former Palazzo degli Anziani (i.e. the Palazzo of the Elders). On one side we see 13th and 14th century houses of great value and palazzo Baldassarri.

We shall now enter the church, which is also called San Michele a Foro or in Foro for the original destination of the piazza's widening (Foro means Court). Built in various stages, it has maintained only a few features of the original building and it immediately shows the signs of the times in which it was touched up: the lower part of the façade is Romanesque, whereas the upper part is Gothic; the bell-tower is from the 12th century, but it was ended in the 19th century. It is made of white limestone, has a very high façade, with a Romanesque statue of Saint Michael dominating from the top. The ornament is particularly suggestive: in the second row from the bottom, beautiful little columns which were radically restored in the last century (some were replaced and taken to the National Museum in Villa Guinigi) are surmounted by portraits of great men of the time, from Garibaldi to Vittorio Emanuele, and so on.

Church of San Michele
1: Interior
2: Madonna delle Grazie (Andrea della Robbia)
3: Crucifix from the school of Lucca (12th century)

46

In the sides there are blind arcades and capitals with particularly interesting corbels and cornices.

The interior is Romanesque, with three aisles and thousands of treasures to see. From the right: on the interior of the façade, a 13th century fresco representing a "Madonna with Child" recently rediscovered; further on, in the corner, Matteo Civitali's Madonna, previously placed on the outer corner of the church and now replaced by a copy; at the first altar, a "Madonna delle Grazie" in glazed terracotta, attributed to Andrea della Robbia, then, on the wall, a "Martirio di Sant'Andrea (i.e. Martyrdom of Saint Andrew)" by Pietro Paolini (Lucca 1435-1525). In the transept, by the main altar, a 12th century crucifix from the Lucchese school, which was moved from the centre of the church where it hung at the beginning of the Presbytery. To the right, a picture of Saints by Filippino Lippi and a high-relief of a Madonna with Child which is believed to

be made of a fragment of a lost funeral monument by Raffaello di Montelupo, dating back to 1522.

In the basement of the apse of the church, outside, we can see three tabernacle windows, decorated with particular pre-Romanesque friezes. These are obviously the lights of the ancient crypt. In connection with this, do not forget that a crypt is to be seen (or believed to exist in origin) in all the main churches in Lucca; but most of them were destroyed during the renovation of the buildings or were interred owing to liturgical changes. These also led to the destruction of ancient choir enclosures Madonna delle Grazie (Andrea della Robbia) which limited part of the central nave (some beautiful fragments of these are kept in the Museum in Villa Guinigi).

Church of San Michele
Four Saints (Filippino Lippi)

CHURCH OF S. SALVATORE

Once you are back in Via Calderia, you can go on up to Piazza del Salvatore or della Misericordia, where you can visit a *neoclassical fountain* built in 1842 and the 12th century *Veglio Tower*, the top of which no longer exists. Then you can move on to the church. Its upper part is in false Ghotic (actually built in the 19th century), but the whole building dates back to before 1180. In the right door there is an interesting architrave with the legend of the golden schyphos. There are three inner naves; on the rights, in the head, an *Ascension* by Zacchia da Vezano and the 15th century Stagi altar, and, on the left, the *Virgin with Saints* by Ardenti.

For those who love music, it might be interesting to have a look at two famous palaces where two renowned musicians were born: *Boccherini* and *Catalani*. The first one is placed in Via Buia, which todat is named after Boccherini, whereas the house of the modern singer of Wally is located in Via degli Asili.

1: The façade; in the foreground
L. Comolli's fountain
2: Lintel of the righthand side lateral door by
Biduino (13 th cent.)

1

2

49

CHURCH OF S. MARIA CORTEORLANDINI

From Piazza San Salvatore we come to Via San Giorgio where, on the right, is the late 16th century Palazzo Boccella, perfectly preserved with its benches along the street, the beautiful windows on the ground floor surmounted by a broken tympanum, and also the grotesque masks on the first floor. From here, turning into the lane opposite the Palazzo, we come to the 17th century façade of the Church of Santa Maria in Corteorlandini (the former Corte Rolandinga), commonly called Santa Maria Nera (i.e. Black Saint Mary) because of the presence of a copy of the Madonna from Loreto. Of the original building (built at the end of the 12th century) we only find the sides and the apses. The interior was completely remade in 1719 with its pulpit, the organ's choir-stalls, the altar and the vaults frescoed and stuccoed by Pietro Scorzini. This very well kept church is probably the most enjoyable among the few examples of Baroque architecture in Lucca. In the passage-way leading to the left side door is a nice polychromatic wood statue of San Nicola da Tolentino attributed to Giacomo Cozzarelli (1453-1515). In the 17th century convent annexed to the church is the State Library, full of rare editions and very valuable illuminated codes.

1: Campanile
2: The inside
3: The lateral portal arc and architrave

PALAZZO ORSETTI

Opposite the side of the church is the 16th century Palazzo Orsetti, today belonging to the Municipality. In the two façades onto Via del Loreto and Via Santa Giustina, two big stone portals open up, pompously engraved in the pillars and in the arch with sphinxes, dragons and grotesque figures: one is surmounted by a mermaid and the other by a Triton. Both the Palazzo an the sculptural decoration are traditionally attributed to Nicolao Civitali. The two entrance passages, covered by a barrel-vault, lead to the porched side of the courtyard (the one from Via Santa Giustina) and to the monumental staircase (the one from Via del Loreto). The pompous 18th century halls on the upper floor with their furniture, tapestries and paintings can be visited. Opposite the palace is a typical garden of Lucca, enclosed in a high wall with windows and covered with plants.

1: A portal
2: The hall of echo
3: The hall of mirrors

ST. AUGUSTINE'S CHURCH

The Convent church is very sober in its aspect.

The lower part of the façade is built in white marble with pilaster strips and a single portal surmounted by an elegant small roof. The upper part is built in fired bricks and is worked in horizontal stripes with a large rose-window in the centre.

On the right side the slender campanile is built on the barrel vault of the ancient **Roman Theatre**, the remains of which can be found nearby. The simple cloister has a portico with slightly ogive arcades supported by brickwork hexagonal columns.

This church was re-built in the 14th century on the remains of a pre-existing sacred building, was then desecrated and used as military stores.

In 1866 the church was brought again into religious use thanks to the commitment of the Holy Spirit Oblate Sisters.

*1: Sant'Agostino campanile (14th cent.).
At the foot of the campanile, the ruins of the Roman Theatre*
2: Ruins of the Tower del Veglio

PALAZZO PFANNER

Palazzo Controni (today known as Pfanner), was built around 1667.

The design of the façade still follows the late 16th century scheme, but the very wide entrance-hall and the pompous staircase resting on pillars and columns opening onto the garden, are already Baroque, yet moderated by the size and the severity typical of the local architectonic tradition. The architect who built this palazzo has not yet been identified. The ingenious and scenographic positioning of the 18th century garden no-doubt recalls the name of Filippo Juvarra who worked in Lucca in those years not only for the completion of the Palazzo Pubblico, but also as the designer of the renovated gardens of some countryside villas. Statues representing the seasons, the months or figures of gods, decorate the octagonal basin and flank the central alley to the lemon-grove with a balustrade surmounted by an eagle and two lions. But the real garden background is represented by the high and thick trees in the wall. The sumptuous garden scenography is perfectly reversible, in the sense that an equally magnificient view can be seen from the walls, therefore having the animated prospect of the palace as a background. In the entrance-hall, which has kept its original brickwork floor, is an 11th century Roman sarcophagus.

In the apartment on the upper floor, decorated with false perspectives by Pietro Scorzini in the first years of the 18th century, in permanent exposition, we see some beautiful local costumes from the 18th century and from the first decades of the following century, bought by or given to the Municipality.

1: The Staircase and the Loggia
2: The garden by day

On pages 54-55
3: The garden by night

53

S. FREDIANO

According to tradition, it was the bishop Frediano himself who in the 6th century founded the primitive church rising in this area, devoting it to San Vincenzo.

It took on the name of San Frediano when, in the 8th century, the remains of the bishop-saint were placed in the cript. The church rose just outside the Roman walls, near the north gate and its façade was turned to the west, as was commonly done at the time. In ancient memoirs it is called "Basilica Langobardorum" and the remaining documents (7th century) confirm the importance it assumed in the Longobard period. In the first half of the 12th century, San Frediano, like almost all the local churches, was rebuilt inside and, for urbanistic reasons, it was positioned in the opposite direction. In the first decades of the following century, it was generally rised (by about 3.30 cm), involving the partial remaking of the apse and the raising of the façade. Furthermore, fragmentary enlargements took place until the 16th century, with the annexion of nearby buildings and the opening of new chapels in the sides. It was consacrated by Pope Eugene III in 1147. In its original state, the church was very different from the way we see it today. The façade was limited in width to three aisles: that means that it was made of the three parts in the centre we see today limited by parastades, excluding the two wings corresponding to the width of the chapels.

Beside the side additions, even the 13th century elevation upset the balance and the proportions; in fact, it was much bigger in the central part, due to the insertion of a large Byzantinesque mosaic. In spite of the changes and additions, the façade of San Frediano is still one of the most authentic examples of local Romanesque. The measured simplicity of the whole and the smoothness of the white hanging without decoration obviously recall the model of the church of Sant'Alessandro. The 13th century restructuring of the interior of the church, on the contrary, led to the creation of a real masterpiece.

On the two splendid original colonnades with twelve identical arches, lie the raised walls of the main nave, interrupted only by a cornice above which the Classical mullioned windows with one light (one in every arcade) open up light and sunny.

It is important to notice that the high rise of the presbytery was introduced subsequently in the 16th century. Being on only one floor, as it was from the start, the great basilica hall certainly appeared even more solemn and deep.

The artist who worked here also remade the apse (bordered by wide white and grey bands) with two rows of mullioned windows with one light and a lintelled loggia.

1

1: The façade large mosaic
2: The façade

56

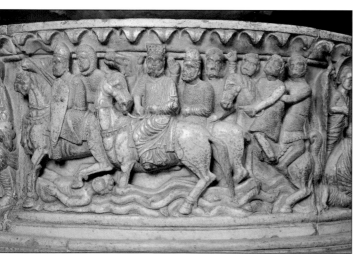

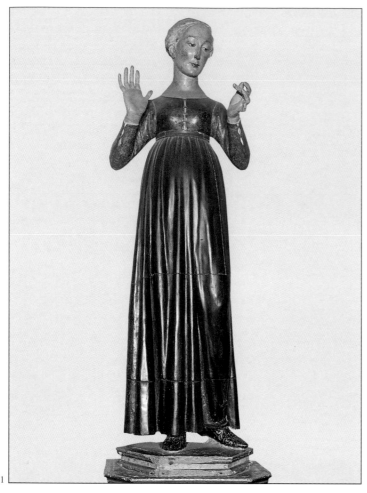

The strong bell-tower - entirely remade in its sheathing in the last century (with mullioned windows with one, two, three and four lights in an upward progression and hanging arches on each level) - follows a very common scheme throughout the area of Lucca. As we said before, the side chapels were built at different times, between the 13th and the 16th century. The most ancient enlargement was done in the year 200, when the church was connected with colonnades to the old Santa Croce Chapel, near its south façade, and to the Baptistery, probably dating back to the 10th century, on the opposite side. Somebody suggests that the two colonnades

and the initial part of the outer wall to the south are the beginning of a project (to enlarge the church to five naves), which was never finished. On entering from the main door, on the right, beyond the second colonnade, you see the magnificent Romanesque baptismal font which was ruined at the end of the 18th century but recently recomposed (1952) on the basis of a drawing representing it as we see it today. Made during the middle of the 12th century, it is in the shape of a circular basin, with a large inner bowl sustained by a pillar and covered by a lid on small columns. In the complex structural decoration we can clearly distinguish the interven-

tion of three different personalities. The most distinct is that of the (certainly) Lombard maestro who engraved the "Storie di Mosè (i.e. Stories of Moses)" on four of the six panels forming the basin's outer pannelling. Narrated in a vivid and simple language, the episodes follow on crowded with figures, without any architectonic structure to frame them in or to divide them.

Church of San Frediano
1: *Polychrome wooden statue of the Virgin of the Annunciation by Matteo Civitali (15 th cent.)*
2: *Baptismal Font - Detail of the basin*
3: *Andrea della Robbia, The Annunciation (15th century)*
4: *Baptismal Font*

The "Passage through the Red Sea", with the Pharaoh's soldiers coming forwards through the waves in their surcoats and helmets like Medieval soldiers, is exceptionally beautiful. To the second artist - a certain Maestro Roberto who left his signature on the side of the basin: "Me fecit Robertus magister in arte peritus" - we owe the "Good Shepherd" and the six Prophets engraved in the two remaining panels aroun the basin. The Byzantine influence evident in the slim figures and the small arches around them (inspired by Roman sarcophaguses), distinguish it deeply from the author of the "Storie di Mosè". The third artist, from Tuscany but with strong Classical touches, worked at the decoration of the central bowl. Engraved on the lid, divided into two overlapping bands, are the Apostles (on top) and the symbols of the months (below). Our eye is attracted by the beautiful masks on the bowl, from which the water flowed, and the pillar decorated with a stylized representation of flowing water, from which a marine monster and a naked child emerge. Although this work is partly deteriorated, it is one of the most prestigious pieces the Romanesque sculpture has left Lucca. At the bottom of the church are some fragments of 13th century frescos, recently detached from the inner wall of the façade (other very ruined frescos from the same period are visible on some columns and on the wall of the main nave). The polychromatic wooden statue ("Maria Annunciata") in the corner, is by Matteo Civitali (1475 circa).

Church of San Frediano
1: The incorrupted body of St. Zita Virgin
*   (1218-1278)*
2: Chapel Trenta - Madonna with Child
*   (Jacopo della Quercia)*
3: Chapel of St. Augustine - Transportation
*   of the Holy Face (Amico Aspertini 1508-9)*

On the wall near the font is a large lunette with a glazed terracotta "Annunciazione" attributed to Andrea della Robbia. To the same artist we also attribute the figure of Saint Bartholomew placed on the pillar dividing the nearby chapel where the remains of Santa Zita are kept (she died in 1278 and was quoted by Dante in the 21st canto of the Inferno). An ancient poetic legend was created around the figure of the saint, immediately adored by the people. Working as a maid for the noble Fatinelli family, one day her master caught her while she was taking some bread she had stolen from her master's cupboard to the poor. When she was asked what she was carrying in her overall, she answered: roses and flowers. Her master did not believe her, but when he had a look, he saw nothing but flowers instead of bread. The miracle is remembered every year in the month of April with the blessing of the newly bloomed daffodils. In those days the piazza and the streets near the church are transformed into an immense garden. Continuing along the nave, on the left wall of the Chapel of San Biagio (the Chapel of Sant'Agostino - Traslation of the Holy Face (Amico Aspertini 1508-9) first), we see a painting of the "Deposition" by Pietro Paolini (1603-1681), dramatically animated by light and foreshortening effects. On the outer part of the Chapel, towards the font, lies a fragmentary altar of the Sacrament by Matteo Civitali (1489), later on dismembered and partly rebuilt.

In the last chapel, in front of the altar, in the big niche in carved and painted wood, we see an "Assunzione" made by Masseo Civitali at the beginning of the 16th century. At the end of the nave to the right is the entrance to the Vestry and to the Opera rooms, where valuable works and sacred decorations are kept: among these are: an enameled copper reliquiary from the Renanan 12th century school, found in 1948 inside Saint Richard's sarcophagus in perfect state of conservation; a bronze falcon, probably originally meant as a censer, a rare work of Medieval Arab art (it used to be on the spire of the façade, where today we find a copy); finally, the entire hangings made of brocatelle produced in Lucca in the 16th century, with which the columns, the walls of the main nave and the apse still today are covered during festivities. Behind the main altar we can see the remains of a magnificient Cosmatesque floor (12th century), brought here when the ancient choir enclosure in which it lay was destroyed to raise the presbytery. The big limestone monolith at the top of the left nave most probably comes from the Anfitheatre. Almost all the church's columns come from Roman monumental buildings; in fact, not only are they made of different materials, but they also have a slightly different diameter, are slightly higher, and their base is thicker (the base and many capitals are also from the Roman period). Near the monolith is the covering plate of the lost Roman sarcophagus previously containing the remains of the bishop San Frediano, an important figure, yet not well defined, in the history of the local church. Tradition attributes him the creation of the Diocese system and the founding of the most important churches in town. Among the works of art kept in San Frediano we immediately notice the beauty of the altarfrontal of the Trenta Chapel(the last in the left nave) by Jacopo della Quercia.

Church of San Frediano - Chapel of St. Augustine
1-3: Amico Aspertini, 16th century. The transport of the Holy Face (details)
2: Miracle of S. Frediano (Amico Aspertini 1508-9)
4: Nativity (Amico Aspertini 1508-9)

In the shape of a Gothic polyptych, in its centre is the "Madonna with Child" and in the four side compartments Sant'Orsola, San Lorenzo, San Girolamo and San Riccardo; in the predella is a bas-relief: in the centre a Pietà with two Sorrowful figures, and at the sides are images of the miracles and the martyrdom of the above mentioned saints. This work, signed in the base of the throne of the Madonna, is dated 1422, but it was probably started long before, as it seems from the differences in language used for the scenes on the predella, which is very dramatic, as well as the upper part, maybe referable to a precedent phase of the artist's activity.

Under the altar is a 3rd century Roman urn containing the ashes of the Irish Saint Richard, who died as a pilgrim in Lucca in 722. In the floor lie the earth-tombs of Lorenzo Trenta and his wife, engraved in bas-relief with the figures of the dead by Jacopo della Quercia in 1416. Although they are very ruined, they are still very interesting. On the front part of the altar is a beautiful "Concezione di Maria (i.e. Mary's Conception)" painted on commission by Francesco Francia in 1511. Descending the left aisle, near the side entrance, we find the Chapel of Sant'Agostino, entirely frescoed in 1508-09 by Amico Aspertini. Vasari considered it to be one of the most beautiful works by the painter from Bologna. The frescos represent: in the two right panels, a Nativity and a miraculous deviation of the Serchio river caused by San Frediano; in the ones on the left, Sant'Ambrogio christening Sant'Agostino and the traslation from Luni to Lucca of the Holy Face which, according to tradition, was originally placed here (in the above mentioned Chapel of Santa Croce); in the vault, on a pale-blue background, is God the Father surrounded by Prophets and Sibyls; in the big lunettes is the approval of the rule of Sant'Agostino and a "Deposition of Christ". The "Last Judgement" on the lunette on the background wall was lost. Vasari says that the noble figures in the "Miracle of San Frediano" and in the "Christening of Sant'Agostino" are "portraits of people signalled in that town (Lucca)". Among these is the self-portrait of the author. In the background we see deep landscapes with the port of Luni, the town of Lucca and imaginative views of Roman ruins and Medieval towers. Even the monochromatic decoration of the fake partition pillars is very interesting; the decoration itself frames figures of saints and scenes from the life of Christ in the entrance arch of the Chapel. Amico Aspertini is also the author of the central fresco, whose colour is very much ruined and which is to the right of the main door with a Madonna on a high stand among four saints and an angel playing the lute. The fresco on the left representing a Visitation is attributed to the "Maestro del Tondo Lathrop". Near the church of San Frediano on the north side was the ancient Cemetery of Santa Caterina, partly

destroyed in the 15th century. On part of it rises a i.e. Chapel of Aid at the bottom of which are still some interesting Medieval tombs.

Walking through the 16th century cloister of the big convent next to the church, we come to the courtyard in which two mullioned windows with three lights and a mullioned window with five lights from the 14th century have been brought out together with frescos from the same period. In the 16th century, when Pietro Martire Vermigli was the prior, the convent of San Frediano became Lucca's main centre of diffusion of the reformist doctrines. The Republic was at first extremely tollerant of the new ideas, which rapidly spread not only among the dominant classes but also throughout the country-side, especially in the Serchio Valley and in Garfagnana. Then, to avoid external intervention which would have endangered its independence, it was forced to forbid the introduction into the State of books declared heretical and then the main representatives of the Reform were banned. Most of them seeked refuge in Geneva, where some of their descendants still live today. The Republic though always managed to obstruct the presence of Inquisition and of the Jesuits in Lucca.

Church of San Frediano
1: Francesco Antonio Cecchi, 19th century. Virgin Mary's Nativity
2: Apse and campanile
3: Bernardino Nocchi, 19th century, St. Anne's death

THE ANFITHEATRE

The Roman Anfitheatre, which today is interred by about three metres, was built outside the walls in the 1st or 2nd century. It has an elliptic shape, and on the outside it had two rows of arches on pillars sustaining the cavea formed by 24 steps.

The big building, gone to rack and ruin during the Barbaric invasions, for centuries was a sort of quarry for building materials. All the columns and the internal marble sheathing were removed and ended up in newly built churches.

On the remaining ruins (the Medieval name "alla Grotta" survives still today in a shop and an inn in that area), houses and other very modest buildings were crammed, but since they used the basement and the structures of the old building, they kept the original shape.

The exceptional piazza we see today was built in 1830 with the ingenious urbanistic intuition of the architect Lorenzo Nottolini; he demolished the buildings inside the arena and united the ground floor with the uninterrupted circular line of houses, leaving the variety of façades unaltered. The overall effect is really astonishing.

Only a few original elements stick out, especially on the east side, where there is the only entrance arch left (the other three entrances are from the last century).

1: The Amphitheatre seen from above

Page 69
2-3-4: The Roman Anfitheatre - details

1

66

VIA FILLUNGO

It is the promenade that the inhabitants of Lucca prefer. It crosses the city from north to south and passes through several streets and squares.

The Chiasso Barletti is particulary evocative. It leads you to Via S. Lucia, with its typical T-shaped shops, irregular façades and roofs that at a certain point almost touch.

Of the numerous towers there were in Lucca in the Middle Ages, the only one left rises at the end of this lane, the Tor dell'Ore (i.e. the Tower of the Hours), in ancient times called Tor della Lite (i.e. the Tower of the Quarrel). About 130 tower have been identified or at least documented, but it seems there were many more. The municipality's laws set a limit to their hight because of some disastrous falls and also to try and stop the ambitions and struggles for power among families and factions. Most of them were demolished with the banishment of their owners, especially in the times of Castruccio who used the materials to build the Augusta fortress.

The Tor dell'Ore probably owes its survival to the fact that for centuries it contained a public clock. To the right, down Via Fillungo (one of the most typical and popular town streets) we come to a short widening where we find the church of San Cristoforo.

1: Via Fillungo
2: Corner between Via S. Andrea and Via Fillungo; in the background the Guinigi Tower
3: Tower of Hours

CHURCH OF S. CRISTOFORO

This 12th and 13th century church is divided into three aisles by two rows of rectangular-based pillars and by four columns sustaining a larger arch. There is an interesting 14th century fresco with a Madonna, at whose feet there is a tombstone to remember two of Matteo Civitali's sons who died young; the artist himself is buried inside the church. The church of San Cristoforo is particularly important to the town's history because it was the seat of the Università dei Mercanti (i.e. the Merchants' University) in the 13th century. Beside the main entrance we can still today see two iron bars placed by the Consuls as a "measure" for the embroidery reeds. Inside, in the 15th century, there were many ornaments which were then removed.

Church of San Cristoforo

PALAZZO CENAMI

Continuing beyond the church, at the cross-roads with Via Santa Croce - still called "Canto d'Arco" - in the corner we see Palazzo Cenami, built around 1530. In the two façades joined in an acute corner, the strong features of the architectonic elements stick out, unusually vast and complex on the ground floor. Unusual for Lucca is the strong stone basement with a torus cornice, the rays of ashlars on the cellar windows and the wide benches along the street (considerably rised compared to the road level). The palazzo has a nice rectangular courtyard with a loggia on all four sides.

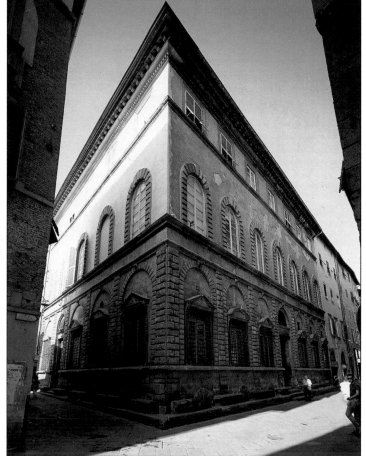

Palazzo Cenami

CHURCH OF S. GIUSTO

Down Via Cenami we come to Piazza San Giusto, unfortu
nately disfigured together with the neighbouring Via Bec
cheria by a despicable building which rises on the area o
an entire ancient district, considerably demolished in
recent times. The citizens immediately called this buildin
"il Palazzaccio (i.e. ugly building)" because its shapeles
dimension weighs upon the delightful little Romanesqu
façade of San Giusto, whose main door is decorated by
large lintel carved in pinewood (12th-13th century). O
the south side of Piazza San Giusto, approximately on th
area previously occupied by the residence of the Longobar
dukes, is Palazzo Gigli. It was built at the beginning of th
16th century and it is the most ancient example in Lucc
of palace with central courtyard and loggia; upon thi
palazzo, many others were modelled. The refined elegance
of the ornamental sculptures, especially in the portal, lea
us to believe they were made by Nicolao Civitali. On th
neighbouring Piazza San Giovanni rises the high garder
wall with its beautiful country-style portal and windows.

Church of San Giusto

PALAZZO BERNARDINI

We now turn left down Via del Battistero (well-known fo
its numerous antique-dealers) and come to the 14th centu
ry portal of the Baptistery (above mentioned together wit
the church of San Giovanni standing next to it); then w
turn left, down the Medieval Via del Gallo and we come t
Piazza Bernardini, in front of the homonymous palazzo
The central part of the palazzo, recognizable by the bench
es along the road, was built between 1517 and 1523 an
originally had mullioned windows with two lights along th
first floor. The widening on the two sides was carried out i
the 18th century, thus respecting the project of the mos
ancient part. Even the opening onto the piazza dates bac
to this time. Except for the ancient lanterns, the palace ha
also kept the beautiful wrought-iron fan-window in th
door and two lovely knockers in the shape of a Moor
head. In the first window right of the door we can see th
so-called "Pietra del miracolo (i.e. Stone of the miracle)"
It is called like this because one of the jambs suddenly ber
as if it was made of wood. According to the people's belie
the stone refused to adhere to the wall, because in ancier
times there used to be a sacred image, which was late
removed to build the palace. Another remarkable 16t
century building is palazzo Balbani, on the opposite side o
the piazza.

Palazzo Bernardini

PALAZZO GUINIGI

Walking away from Piazza Bernardini from the east side, we turn left into Via Sant'Anastasio. Where it meets Piazza del Suffragio, we find the Oratorio di Santa Giulia with its 14th century marble façade. The brick apse-area overlooking the characteristic Vicolo del- l'Altopascio is more ancient. In the alley to the right off Via Santa Croce we can still see the remains of the Magione dei Cavalieri dell'Altopascio (Mansion of the Altopascio Knights), also called, for their symbol, Cavalieri del Tau (Knights of the Tau). This ordere is probably the most ancient of the religious-military orders (it was founded in the 10th century); its duty was assistance to pilgrims and therefore also service and security of the roads. Its greatest flourishing occurred in the 12th and 13th century, when its centres were spread all over Europe. Walking down Via Sant'Anastasio we soon get to the sweet little church bearing the same name: a small Romanesque building in red brick, enlivened by borders and ashlars in white limestone. In the interior, renovated with barrel-vaults in the 16th century, on the left wall we see a large painting representing the Circumcision, a remarkable work signed and dated by Jacopo Ligozzi (1594). Following along the side of the church and then turning left, we finally come to Via Sant'Andrea at the foot of Palazzo Guinigi's famous tower full of trees.

Built at the end of the 14th century, the palazzo is the last aulic rielaboration of the traditional local Romanesque-Gothic house. Like the tower, it is completely made of bricks, and on the ground floor it has original open arches resting on stone pillars. On the upper floors, wide windows with three and four lights, with trefoil arches on thin little columns, give light to the halls, making the compact wall much lighter. Since the Guinigi family extinguished, the palazzo recently passed over to the Town Council: we therefore hope it will soon be completely restored. The tower is open for the public to visit.

Opposite, on Via Guinigi, rises another similar palazzo, originally belonging to the same family and also standing next to a tower, whose remains are to be seen in the corner on the right.

The two buildings, with the small closed loggia in the corner of Via Sant'Andrea, the garden wall made of brick and the grey-stone façade of the nearby church of Santi Simone e Giuda (13th century) are among the most stimulating and better kept buildings in town.

1: The Guinigi Tower
2: Tower and Palazzo Guinigi

CHURCH OF S. MARIA BIANCA

From Via Guinigi we come to Via dell'Angelo Custode which leads us, to the right, in the square in which lies the church of Santa Maria Forisportam, so called because in ancient times it rose outside the perimeter of the Roman walls. Today it is known as Santa Maria Bianca.

Built between the end of the 12th century and the beginning of the 13th, in the façade it repeats the Pisan scheme of the superimposed rows of small loggias, with blind arches below continuing together in the sides, in the transepts and in the apse.

The white marble hangings, typical of the Romanesque style in Lucca, leads it back to the local tradition.

The three portals on the façade are richly engraved in the lintels, in the corbels and cornices with Classical motives: the left lintel with a lion and a snout is particularly remarkable.

The church lacks a base because it was interred by about a metre and a half from the time it was built.

The three-aisle interior is Romanesque, but the main nave and the transept were raised with brick walls and covered with vaults in the 16th century. In that time the crypt was demolished, but we can still see the small windows in the basement of the apse.

Only one engraved and inlaid tile of the Presbyterial enclosure has remained and it is kept in the National Museum.

The Romanesque column in granite which rises isolated in the centre of the square used to indicate the end of the Palio run during the festivities until the end of the 18th century.

Church of Santa Maria Forisportam

74

CHURCH OF S. MARIA DELLA ROSA

We now leave the piazza walking southwards down Via della Rosa at the end of which, near the walls, we find the small church of Santa Maria della Rosa. The two mullioned windows with two lights and the door, dated 1309, were originally the façade of an oratory later annexed to the church, rebuilt in 1333. Besides the two mullioned windows, the side overlooking the road presents four windows with four lights included in large round arches. Even here, like elsewhere in Lucca, the Gothic taste is expressed with ornamental motives. The façade, without its marble panelling, is decorated with a portal from the school of Matteo Civitali.

The 15th century interior is divided into three aisles by elegant columns. On the left side we still see part of the Roman walls (2nd century bC). Walking back shortly, we turn right, down Via del Giardino Botanico. The district rising south of the road was built ex novo in the 16th century, after this area was included in the new city walls. These are generally minor yet decent buildings, however there are some remarkable buildings such as Palazzo Poggi on the corner with Via della Rosa. Near this lies the urban villa of the Arnolfini family with its porched courtyard opposite the façade, closed by a wall with windows. At the end of the road is the entrance of the Giardino Botanico (i.e. Botanical Gardens), founded by Maria Luisa di Borbone in 1820.

With its century-old plants, the small lake and the artificial mountain, the gardens have the noble aspect of a mansion park. Inside its enclosure is the access to the dungeons of the nearby Baluardo di San Regolo (i.e. Bulwark of San Regolo).

Church of Santa Maria della Rosa

VIA DEI FOSSI

So called for the ditch running in the centre of it and dividing it lengthwise, Via dei Fossi is one of the most suggestive streets in town. For two thirds, from the Botanical Gardens to the Madonna dello Stellario, it runs along the outside perimeter of the Medieval walls, of which there still is a majestic gate devoted to the two Saints Gervasio and Protasio, commonly called "Portone dell'Annunziata". Made of grey sandstone bordered by white limestone and originally decorated with sculptures (now lost) it is flanked by two semi-circular towers, whose crenellation has also been destroyed. Next to the south tower rises the small church of Santa Maria Annunziata or "dell'Alba (i.e. of Dawn)" with its pretty Renaissance porch. On the bridge in front of the door we can see a small Neoclassical fountain, created with some others when Lorenzo Nottolini finished building Maria Luisa's new acqueduct to bring the water into town from the mountains around Pisa. Along Via dei Fossi, on the right, we see the wall around the garden of Villa Buonvisi whose main entrance opens to the south, onto Via Elisa. The 16th century building is the example upon which various other local villas were modelled at the time. In the basement there are the bathroom and kitchen, whereas on the rised level there is a staircase leading to the garden; and then there is the attic with its panoramic loggia, originally open from side to side. Particularly beautiful is the rear side, opening onto the garden with a large loggia. At the bottom of the garden, in axis with the villa, is the beautiful portal leading to the Ninfeo (i.e. a small temple devoted to the cult of the Nymphs), made of four couples of columns and surmounted by a balustrade with two statues of rivers. Always in axis with the villa, and therefore inserted in the general project of the garden, lies the church of the Santissima Trinità (i.e. Holy Trinity), built in 1589 in front of the entrance onto Via Elisa

The loggia and the halls on the upper floor were frescoed with mythological and allegoric figures by Ventura Salimbeni immediately after his departure from Rome in 1593. Illusionistic squarings harmoniously include the compositions in the architectonic scheme, whereas the serene grace and the chromatic brightness of the paintings enliven the halls. In the other walls enclosing the garden (onto Via dei Fossi, Via Elisa and Via Santa Chiara) there are portals and windows bearing the Ammannati touch. The villa, now property of the Government, has recently been perfectly restored. After Villa Buonvisi we procede along Via dei Fossi to the column of the Madonna dello Stellario, erected in 1687 by Giovanni Lazzoni. In the base there is the engraving of a sight of Lucca, which is very interesting because it represents Porta San Donato with the raised road over the ditch, the drawbridge and the half-moons in front of the bulwark, already covered by trees. A scroll ornament bears the writing: "Vere libera serva nos liberos".

1-3: Two views of Via dei Fossi
2: Villa Buonvisi, later Villa Bottini
4: Madonna dello Stellario; in the background St. Francis Church

CHURCH OF SAN FRANCESCO

Turning right in the piazza, we find we are standing in front of the church of San Francesco. It was rebuilt and remarkably enlarged in the 14th century; today its façade bears two blind arcades and a splayed central portal, at the sides of which are two tombs: one from 1249, the other from the middle of the following century. The upper half of the façade is recent (and you can tell!). Along the north side of the church are the cloisters with some Medieval tombs, and the 13th century vestry with a central pillar to hold up the vaults.

Inside (only one nave and three apsal chapels), between the second and the third altar on the right, you can see the funeral monument to the bishop, poet and humanist Giovanni Guidiccioni (1500-1541), an extremely beautiful and interesting work by an unknown artist. The third altar was built by the Università dei Tessitori (i.e. Weavers' University) after the serious upturn of the ragged (1531), which started in this district where all the craftsmen used to work (they used the ditch's current as motive-power in their workshops). In the base of the columns notice the "Torsello" (i.e. bale of raw silk), symbol of the corporation, and up high, the dedication: "Divo Francisco paupertatis amanti depauperata textorum Universitas dicavit". Further on, on the wall, there is a 16th century tombstone in memory of Castruccio Castracani of the Antelminelli family. Near the right chapel, up high, we see the fragments of the demantled monument by Nino Visconti, Judge of Gallura, quoted by Dante in the 8th canto of the Purgatorio. Most of the frescos in the chapel have been lost: among the remaining ones is the beautiful and very well preserved one on the right "Presentazione al Tempio e Sposalizio di Maria (i.e. Mary's Presentation to the Temple and Wedding)", by a 15th century Florentine artist who has not yet been identified for sure. Even the benches in the choir and the book-rest in the major chapel were created in the 15th century by Leonardo Marti. Between the second and the third altar on the left are the tombs of the Lucchese musicians Luigi Boccherini (1743-1805) and Francesco Geminiani (1687-1762).

Church of San Francesco

VILLA GUINIGI

Next to the south side of the church rises Villa Guinigi, the beautiful residence that Paolo Guinigi, Lord of Lucca, had built in the first decades of the 15th century, not far from the Medieval city walls (it was in fact called "Palazzo dei Borghi" (i.e. Suburban Palace), as opposed to the one in town). "Noble palace with a beautiful garden", as Giovanni Sercambi called it in his "Croniche" as he observed that 36,000 florins were spent to build it in a decade and that another 40,000 would have been necessary to finish it. Sercambi also described the party which took place there on the evening of the 7th of August 1420, to celebrate Paolo's wedding. At the fall of the Guinigi family (1430) the villa was confiscated and the precious objects contained in it were lost. The wonderful garden was later isolated and destroyed, whereas the palace, although it was more and more degrading through the years, substantially kept its structure. Today it has been completely restored and it has become the seat of the National Museum. Numerous architects, especially from the North, seem to have been payed for working on the palace, but none of them is specified as director of these works. The palazzo, though, basically refers to the Romanesque-Gothic building tradition in Lucca: see the elongated body with only two façades (the short sides are covered by crenellation); the particular roof with a non-central load-bearing wall; the mullioned windows with three lights with trefoil arches resting on slim little columns, included in round arches (very similar to those in the Guinigi palaces in town). Typical of the local buildings of the earlier centuries is the chromatic encounter between the white columns, the grey stone pillars and the red bricks. However, there are some marks betraying the change in time and in taste: the dimension itself of the building, up to then uncommon for a villa, the smooth solidity of the walls with no longer the traditional stone pillars connected by arches; the uninterrupted series of mullioned windows with three lights on the main façade, aerating almost an entire loggia, the vastness of the double central loggia (eight arcades in front and seven at the back).

The very large garden, whose limits and conformation are well-known (a trace of the alleys is to be found in the road-system of this area), was surrounded by a high crenelled wall: part of it is still connected to the east side of the villa, with its big gate originally surmounted by the Guinigi coat of arms.

Villa Guinigi

79

NATIONAL MUSEUM

The Museum has been conceived in a modern way according to organic and rational criteria, avoiding that an excessive crowding of works of art could prevent visitors from fully appreciating the architecture of this gorgeous villa. All the pieces collected here come from various buildings in town and in the surroundings: therefore, it represents a proof of what masters and craftsmen from Lucca (or working and living in Lucca for some time) created in a millennium. The richness of this collection obviously does not allow us to give a detailed description of it. We will give some general information, referring to the Museum's catalogue. In the opposite garden, on the bottom of a basin, lies a Roman mosaic (a Triton with a Nereid) from the Imperial period (1st century). In the garden to the left, beyond the entrance arch, is a tract of Roman wall in blocks of tufa. In the north loggia are columns, capitals and architraves from the façade of San Michele (13th century). In the two halls on the left are fragments from the Roman period and archaeological pieces, among which are also the ornaments from Ligurian and Etruscan tombs.

On the south loggia see Balduccio Parghia degli Antelminelli's earth - tombstone (1423); although it is very much ruined, it reveals Jacopo della Quercia's style. The other tombstone, Caterina degli Antelminelli's, is believed to be a deed of Jacopo's school. The bronze bells are all signed and dated (13th century). The three halls of the west wing are full of Romanesque, Gothic and Renaissance sculptures. The Romanesque pieces from hall number 3 are particularly interesting: mirrors of ambones and transennas, capitals, lintels and statues from the 8th to the 13th century deriving from churches in Lucca which were destroyed or transformed. The marble high-relief of "Sanson fighting against the lion" by a 12th century local artist, in origin was a tile of the Cathedral's ancient choir enclosure. The Madonna with Child in hall number 5, a beautifully-made bas-relief in coloured and golded marble, used to be in the now destroyed Merchants' Loggia and it is attributed to Matteo Civitali. In the two remaining halls on the ground floor are some 19th century pieces and a series of weights and measures from the Republic of Lucca. Upstairs we come to a sunny hall overlooking the church of San Francesco, through big mullioned windows with three lights. Here we find some important products of woodcraft which was particularly developed in Lucca for centuries. The most ancient piece is an oak cupboard (its two doors are carved with motives of grape shoots), which was probably part of Paolo Guinigi's very rich library, together with three identical others kept in the rooms of the Opera de Duomo. They are almost for sure the deed of the "wood work masters" Arduino and Alberto da Baiso, who worked here in 1413-14 (in 1434, the Republic gave a small writing-desk carved by them to Lionello d'Este). We then see the four inlaid seats made by Leonardo Marti between 1452 and 1457, from the Cathedral's "large choir". From the Cathedral's choir is also the inlay with bust of San Martino

created by Matteo Civitali in 1494. Particular interest is drawn to the backs of the seats in the Cappella degli Anziani in the Palazzo Pubblico, in which in 1529 Ambrogio and Nicola Pucci inlaid a series of views of Lucca, almost all easily recognisable and built with unique perspective knowledge. But the most splendid elements of this series are the cupboard doors (from the vestry in the church of San Martino), made between 1484 and 1488 by Cristoforo Canozzi da Lendinara. The figure of San Martino Vescovo and (most of all) the four wonderful views of cities surrounded by walls and bristling with towers, roofs and bell-towers, as well as buildings with porched bridges and staircases over which dominate hills, clearly reveal the knowledge of the art of Piero della Francesca, a friend of Canozzi's. In the hall we also see a beautiful painting deriving from Siena, a "Visitation" attributed to Giacomo Pacchiarotti (1474-1539 circa). Also notice the oval medallion bearing the profile of Paolo Guinigi, a deed of a 16th century sculptor, and the lantern standing on a wrought iron foot (15th century) from a convent. In the next hall (number 11) we see two Crucifixes: one, from the second half of the 12th century, is among the most ancient works

National Museum
1: View of a hall with exposition
2: The Bishop Saint Martin. Wooden marquetry by Cristoforo Canozzi da Lendinara (15th cent.)
3: Virgin and Infant. Painted and gilted marmor low relief by Matteo Civitali
4: View of the city. Wooden marquetry by Cristoforo Canozzi da Lendinara (15th cent.)

of the Lucchese school; the other, from the first decades of the 13th century, is the only signed work by Berlinghiero, Lucca's most important painter of the time. The third Crucifix, signed and dated, is by the local artist Deodato Orlandi (1288). In this hall there are also the predella of a lost polyptych belonging to Ugolino di Nerida Siena (first half of the 14th century) and two lovely paintings - the Virgin and Saint John the Evangelist - parts of a polyptych which today is spread around various museums, attributed to the artist conventionally known as "Ugolino Lorenzetti". Hall number 12 contains paintings from the 14th and 15th century, among which are a triptych signed by Angelo Puccinelli (second

half of the 14th century) and a 15th century "Madonna with Child" (from the Flemish school). The tabernacle with three shrines in carved wood, golded and partly painted (it used to contain three small statues which now are exposd in hall number 4), is attributed to Priamo della Quercia, Jacopo's son, who worked in the area around Lucca in the first half of the 15th century. This tabernacle, commonly called "dei pimpinnacoli" for its ornate Gothic structure, served as model for the framing of many 15th century polyptychs in this region. In hall number 13 are three works attributed to the "Maestro del Tondo Lathrop", a local painter working at the beginning of the 16th century, whose personality has laboriously

been outlined by the critic on the base of the "Tondo Guinigi" of the Lathrop Collection. Besides echoes of the Ghirlandaio, of Aspertini and most of all of Filippino Lippi, this maestro also reveals a Flemish influence, understandable when we think about the close business relations between Lucca and Flanders. For this reason we see that there were and still are numerous Flemish paintings in the ancient private collections in Lucca. Another local artist from the same period and from the same figurative culture, known as the "Maestro of the Immacolata Concezione", is the author of a painting representing the "Immaculate Conception" and another representing the Coronation of Mary. The two artists most probably are Michele Ciampanti and Antonio Corsi, two remarkable figures in local painting at the end of the 15th century. In hall number 13 there are also a nice triptych from the German school attributed to Martin Heemskerk (1498-1574) and two splendid high-reliefs in polychromatic wood from a big niche, produced in Siena in the second half of the 15th century: Vecchietta sculptured the "Dormizio Verginis" and, at his death in 1480, left the work later called "Madonna Assunta" for his apprentice Neroccio Landi (1447-1500) to finish. In hall number 14 there are two large pictures painted by Frà Bartolomeo in his full maturity: the first is the "Apparition of the Eternal to Saint Mary-Magdalene and to Saint Catherine from Siena" bearing this inscription: "Orate pro pictore 1509" (this is one of the artist's most beautiful works); the second is the "Madonna of Mercy" signed: "1515 F. Bartholomeus pictor fiorentinus". In the same hall there are a "Madonna in Glory with the Extasy of Saint Catherine" (1773) by Pompeo Batoni Saints by Amico Aspertini (1474-1552) and three pictures by Zacchia

1

da Vezzano, the most important local painter in the first half of the 16th century. In the following halls, we can follow the history of painting in Lucca between the second half of the 16th and the following centuries, to the caravaggian (i.e. followers of Caravaggio) Pietro Paolini (1603-1681) and Pompeo Batoni, the great 18th century local painter (1708-1787), whose "Extasy of Saint Catherine", "Martyrdom of Saint Bartholomew" and portrait of the bishop Gian Domenico Mansi (1765) are here exposed. The paintings in this hall are alternated by precious objects of minor art, furniture, wrought iron, inlays and wood carvings. Two 16th century coffers with their complex and "secret" mechanisms (all still functioning) are very interesting. The very rich series of sacred hangings from the 15th to the 18th century are exposed in halls number 16 and 17. In the latter, a small show-case contains very rare Longobard ornaments from the 7th century found in some tombs. Before walking out of the garden we ought to take a look at the fifteen terracotta statues placed in the hedges, which are a typical example of Lucchese 18th century garden sculpture.

National Museum
1: Portrait of the Archbishop Giovan Domenico Mansi (18th c.)
   by Pompeo Batoni
2: Extasy of Saint Catherine (1773) by Pompeo Batoni
3: Virgin and Infant and Saint Sebastian and Saint Rocco (16th cent.)
   by Zacchia il Vecchio
4: Madonna with child between St. Steven and St. Jerome (11th century)
   "Maestro del Tondo Lathrop"

2

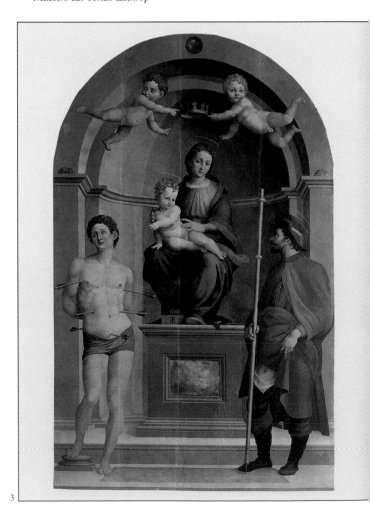

3

AVE GRATIA PLENA

4

S. PIETRO SOMALDI

Having returned to Piazza San Francesco, we come back to the Madonna dello Stellario, next to which is another small Neoclassical fountain. From here you can see the whole of Via dei Fossi, even the last stretch to the north which lacks important architectonic elements but is nevertheless extremely lively. The trees growing from the wall at the two ends of the street are like a background drop. We walk along Via della Fratta, at the end of which, on the right, we enter Piazza San Pietro, a typical Lucchese piazza with an irregular perimeter along which are th[e] Romanesque façade of the church, the houses and palazz[i] from the 16th century, with a garden and a balcony full [of] flowers. The church of San Pietro Somaldi (so calle[d] because of the Longobard name of its founder, Sumuald[o]) was rebuilt at the end of the 12th century. The façade i[n] grey sandstone bordered in white limestone was made i[n] the 13th century and finished off with the rows of sma[ll] loggias probably at the beginning of the following centur[y] together with the upper part of the brick bell-tower.

The beautiful lintel of the main door, dated 1203 and rep[-]resenting the handing over of the keys to Saint Peter, [is] attributed to Guido Bigarelli. The interior is divided int[o] three aisles by rows of pillars; by the first altar on the rig[ht] is an "Assunzione (i.e. Assumption)" dated and marke[d] with a monogram by Zacchia da Vezzano (1532), and b[y] the first altar on the left, a picture with images of Saint[s] doubtedly attributed to Raffaellino del Garbo (1470 circa [-] 1525 circa).

1: Sculpted lintel of the portal representing the handing over of the keys of
   Saint Peter (attributed to Guido Bigarelli)
2: Façade and campanile
3: A suggestive view of the city

3

THE VILLAS IN LUCCA

We have left out the description of works and monuments which did not seem particularly significant to us, although they all have great historic and artistic value.

If we had acted differently, we would have had to walk through all the streets in Lucca, stopping at every step. Nevertheless, we cannot finish this tour without briefly talking about the villas in the countryside, which represent a relevant aspect of the local architecture.

Of the 14th and 15th century villas (among which is Castruccio's in Massa Pisana) we only have some minor examples, generally very much rehashed and in bad condition. But from what is left we can still understand the prevailing typology: with an elongated body and a hut-roof, therefore with only the two façades, usually on two floors, with mullioned windows with two lights.

But the typical Lucchese villa is the one the rich merchant families (later copied also by minor families) started to build themselves at the beginning of the 16th century.

They are mainly at the foot of the hills, not far from town, in a position chosen so as to dominate the plain and yet remain isolated.

The architects who built the merchants' villas are the same who built their palaces in town: the severe and moderate style remains the same.

But whereas in town they usually restored existing buildings and were always limited by insurmountable space and conformation limits, the isolation of the countryside building allowed them complete freedom of planning (yet in full respect of the purchasers' needs) and therefore determined relevant differences as to the shape of the town palazzo.

During the 16th century villas tended to take on more and more the shape of a parallelepiped and therefore also the sides took on architectonic dignity and sober elegance. The most articulate solutions with right-angle wings or advancing bodies are usually suggested by the conformation of the ground.

The inner body, centre of the town palace, never appears and is replaced in its functions by a loggia on the rear as well as by the central hall on the upper floor, around which are the rooms.

The kitchen and bathrooms are in the basement, whereas the attic floor (sometimes there is a belvedere or a roof-terrace above it) is used as lodging for the servants as well as pantry and wardrobe.

Country-style buildings are usually at hand, because villas are not only pleasant places to stay in, but also and most of all they are the place where farms are cautiously managed and where agricultural work is promoted: the type of work which has slowly transformed the hills around Lucca in wonderfully built and tidy space; unfortunately, today this area is being ruined.

The vast fenced area is divided in regular sectors destined to garden, vegetable-garden and fruit-orchard: the water from the brooks fills the basins, fountains and jets.

The main avenue, with its noble access portal, is in axl with the villa and continues on the back of the building to the beginning of the woods.

Of course, many of these villas underwent more or less radical transformation in the 17th and 18th century. The façades were livened up, according to the Baroque taste, with staircases, loggias and terraces decorated with statues whereas the gardens abandoned their classical "Italian" form and took on a more animated and scenographic aspect. At the beginning of the 19th century the parks of the main villas were partly changed into "English" gardens.

Among the many villas that would deserve mentioning, we have to restrain to only the few that are normally open to the public: Villa Reale in Marlia, Villa Mansi in Segromigno, Villa Torrigiani in Camigliano and Villa Garzoni in Collodi.

The first three are at the foot of the Pizzorne mountain, about ten km north of Lucca, not far from one another. The last, Villa Garzoni, is a bit further away, near Pescia.

1

VILLA REALE

The antique Villa Reale in Marlia was entirely rebuilt in the 17th century with its garden and the nearby Palazzina dell'Orologio. Prints and drawings of the period witness its noble late-Renaissance aspect.

In 1811 Elisa Baciocchi, princess of Lucca for Napoleon's wish, forced the owners, the Orsetti family, to give her the villa, with the ambition of transforming it into something really royal.

The aspect of the house was totally changed and the interior radically remade with a new distribution of the rooms, refinedly decorated and furnished in Neoclassical style. The garden was enormously enlarged (in the project it should have been even bigger), including the nearby 16th century Villa del Vescovo.

The new entrance was really Napoleonic: two small buildings and a semi-circular courtyard limited by hedges and big marble vases. In the arrangement of the park, though, the architectonic relevant 17th century parts were respected: the scenographic basin with the water-theatre behind the villa, the splendid lemon-grove with the fish-pond and the unique vegetable-theatre. The geometrically trimmed and by now very high yew-hedges characterize this part of the garden.

The great innovation is the enlarging and prolonging of the lawn in front of the villa "designed and planned by a very skilful English landscapist".

The lawn gradually descends towards a small lake surrounded by woods of plants wisely chosen for their shape, colour and disposition. The sight, with the light playing magic effects between the trees at different times of the day, is incredibly beautiful. In a letter to his sister, the prince of Metternich, who like other important people was a guest in the villa, called it "a really divine place".

It is also worth remembering that in his memoirs Nicolò Paganini at length talks about the concerts he played here, since he was a "bedroom virtuoso" and orchestra director of Elisa's.

1: Villa Bernardini

Villa Reale
2: Piazzale in front of Villa Reale, meeting point for guided tours

2

VILLA MANSI

Built in the second half of the 16th century, Villa Mansi was enlarged and transformed in its façade by Maurizio Oddi around 1635. In the next century the abbot Gian Francesco Giusti further elaborated the façade by changing the upper part and adding statues and balustrades. The difference in interventions, though, is not noticeable in the prospect of the villa, which is light, animated and sunny although it has kept its original structure. Even the big 16th century garden had relevant changes done to it in the two following centuries and then even during the 19th century. The east side with star-shaped avenues, the big basin and the Palazzina dell'Orologio are all deeds of a clever architect of French origin from the 18th century. The west part was planned and built between 1725 and 1732 with a double scenographic garden by Filippo Juvarra, who also took care of the water system (as we mentioned before, Juvarra is the creator of many drawings and design of local villas, which only in part were then built).

At the beginning of the 19th century the biggest part of the park with gardens designed by Juvarra was demolished so as to adopt the "natural" or "English" type, in which the 18th century remains took on a different aspect and meaning. This complex is for sure one of the most remarkable in the whole region around Lucca.

VILLA TORRIGIANI

Villa Torrigiani in Camigliano is also from the second half of the 16th century and was enlarged and completely transformed in its prospect during the first decade of the 18th century by Alfonso Torregiani (the original loggia still exists on the rear of the building).

Animated by projections and indents and by the colour contrast between the yellow tufa, the grey stone and the white statues and busts, the façades appears exceptionally animated and pompous.

Equally superb and sumptuous is the big portal leading to the garden, placed at the end of a 700 m. long avenue through the fields flanked by two rows of very high cypress trees. Outside the wall, on one side is the chapel and on the other is a small Medieval village.

Even the unique stairs on an elliptic plan, inside, as well as the rich decoration of the central hall, date back to the beginning of the 18th century.

In spite of the changes in the last century, the garden, dominated by the grand façade of the palace, has partly kept its 18th century structure made of two basins with a slightly raised border and the symmetrical side arrangement of the plants. On the rear, the gardens are all placed around a big round basin.

The part of the park on the right hand side of the villa is very complex and varied, with its green gallery decorated

3

with statues and fountains, the big fish-pond, Flora's secret garden and the most beautiful Ninfeo (i.e. small fountain devoted to the adoration of the Nymphs) enriched by water effects which are probably the most elaborate in Italy, very much admired since they were built.

Villa Mansi
1-2: Views of the Villa and of the 18th garden of Diana

Villa Torrigiani
3-4: Views of the Villa and of the 18th garden

4

PESCIA

Pescia is a delightful small town renowned mainly for its great *Flower Market*, the biggest in the whole of Tuscany. In the past it was also a great centre for the production of special paper for the publishing trade and for the printing of banknotes.

Its historic centre is typically Medieval and so are the lovely *Cathedral* and *Palazzo Pretorio (i.e. Praetorial Palace)*.

1: Pescia: Piazza Mazzini
2: The stream Pescia

Collodi - Pinocchio's Park
3: Pinocchio and the Fairy

Villa Garzoni
4: Aerial view of the Park

VILLA GARZONI

Villa Garzoni in Collodi was entirely rebuilt in the first decades of the 17th century and it is the greatest "palazzo in villa" of the region with its four floors, central completion, base on the terraced slope, the access flights of stairs, the bombastic portal and its two guard-houses on either side of the wide façade.

The village of Collodi seems to be huddled up and hidden behind the villa, on the top of the hill: until not long ago, in fact, the inhabitants used to go through the palace gates to reach their village. On entering, the visitor is struck by the unexpected appearance of the delightful "summer palace" (beyond the portico and the courtyard), based on a design by Filippo Juvarra made in the first decades of the 18th century.

The small Baroque building with a movement in the curvilinear prospect, the pretty pattern of volutes and the colourism of the materials used, all clearly contrast with the solemnity of the palace.

The interior has kept the stucco and fresco decoration, and partly also the fittings from the 17th and 18th century. Originally the villa had only a terraced garden on the right side, which now has become a little forest. The main garden, completely independent and not in axle with the building, was built a little later, towards the middle of the 17th century. Beyond the vast semi-circular entrance with two round basins limited by wavy hedges, the main garden was obtained by geometrically terracing the steep slope of the hill and obtaining a "water staircase" sided by caves, niches, statues and balustrades. In the years 1786-87 Ottaviano Diodati, an aristocrat from Lucca, re-elaborated the structure by enriching it with new inventions and perspectives, by making the water-show grander and more pompous and by filling the hedges and avenues with Naturalistic brickwork statues.

In the garden, beyond the 17th century Ninfeo and the Vegetable-Theatre, we can see the Labyrinth made of hedges and water effects; this is the only one left in the villas in Lucca.

3

4

93

1

TORRE DEL LAGO

Torre del Lago is a small village between Lucca and Viareggio which owes its fame to the great composer Giacomo Puccini, who built a pretty villa along the shores of the Massaciuccoli lake, where he composed most of his works. Today the villa has been turned into the *Museo Pucciniano (i.e. Puccini Museum)* with the Maestro's tomb in a hall used as Chapel. Every year, in the summer, Torre del Lago hosts the open-air *Festival Pucciniano*, during which the musician's most important works are represented.

2

1-2: Aerial views of the lake of Massaciuccoli

VIAREGGIO

Viareggio is Versilia's most popular seaside resort with its beautiful beach full of Italian and foreign tourists who also come here for Carnival to see the enormous carts parading through town.

Beautiful avenues lined with palmtrees, oleanders and Mediteranean plants run through the residential area placed between the grand Apuane Alps and the sea, in two huge pine-forests.

The very large port of Viareggio contains most of Tuscany's fishing flotilla and many shipyards in which boats are built and exported around the world. What remains of the Medieval city is only the *Torre Matilde (i.e. Matilde Tower)* built in 1534 within a fortified system for the defence of the port. The most important monuments in town date back to the end of the 19th-beginning of the 20th century; among these we recall the *Teatro Margherita (i.e. Margherita Theatre)*, the *Palazzo delle Muse (i.e. Palace of the Muses)*, the seat of the *A.C. Blanc Museum* and the *Bagno Balena*.

1: The promenade and the Margherita Theatre
2: The entrance to the port
3: The beach
4: Carnival

THE GARFAGNANA AREA AND THE LIMA VALLEY

The Garfagnana area extends along most of the course of the Serchio river, flowing between the two chains of the Apuane Alps and of the Apennines; since these mountains are very different from one another, we can say that this territory has a unique landscape. This area lies in the northern part of Tuscany on the border to Luigiana and to the Emilia Apennine.

Although it was inhabited by Ligurians and Romans in very ancient times, Garfagnana gained historic importance only from the times of Matilde di Canossa; due to the division of the area among various Seignories in those days, in fact, new connections had to be established between Emilia and the Tyrrhenian Sea, in alternative to the plains.

The villages, the monasteries, the castles, the parishes and the bridges scattered all over the territory are typically Medieval and they are particularly attractive to the tourists, who in Garfagnana can satisfy their wish to live in nature and admire the work of man in the course of the centuries.

BORGO A MOZZANO

Coming from Lucca, along the Brennero state road, the first town we meet is Borgo a Mozzano, a typically Medieval village characterized by the *Ponte della Maddalena (i.e. Magdalene's Bridge)*, commonly known as the *Ponte del Diavolo (i.e. Devil's Bridge)* because the legend says it was built by the Evil in only one night. This ecceptional bridge, with its asymmetrical arches and its peculiar shape, was probably ordered by the Countess Matilde di Canossa and built during the 14th century.

BAGNI DI LUCCA

The charming town of Bagni di Lucca, made up of numerous fractions developing along the Lima river, is well-known for its Thermal baths, which were famous already in the 11th century. The town's greatest name was reached at the beginning of the 19th century because this is where the Lucchese nobility used to invite all the European aristocrates as well as the most famous artists such as Montaigne, Byron, Shelley, D'Azeglio and Carducci.

The success, even today, of the Thermal baths is due to the high temperature and the radioactivity of the water. Plunged in nature and surrounded by magnificent Luccese style villas, Bagni di Lucca is really a beautiful place to see.

: Borgo a Mozzano: the Devil's Bridge
: Monti di Villa
-4: Bagni di Lucca: View and the Lima river
: Bagni di Lucca: Ponte a Serraglio
   on the Lima river
: Castelvecchio Pascoli: portrait of the poet by
   Cordati, in Barga's Town Hall
: Castelvecchio Pascoli: the poet's house

BARGA

Placed at the top of a high hill, Barga is a lovely Medieval village dominated by its *Cathedral*.

The city centre, surrounded by walls, is characterized by narrow and steep alleys along which rise beautiful buildings. In the Middle Ages Barga was famous for producing and trading silk.

The modern part of this small town is placed more towards the valley and is called *Il Giardino* (*i.e. The Garden*).

Barga
1: View
2: Cathedral
3: Cathedral - Pulpit

CASTELNUOVO GARFAGNANA

Castelnuovo Garfagnana is the most important village in this area and the seat of the *Comunità Montana (i.e. Mountain Comunity)* made of 16 Municipalities. Placed at the confluence between the Turrite Secchia and the Serchio rivers, this small town has a Medieval structure and is dominated by the 12th century *Rocca Ariostesca (i.e. Fortress of Ariosto)*, so called because the great poet Ludovico Ariosto stayed here when the Estensis were the Lords of Castelnuovo.

LE PANIE

Le Panie is one of the major massifs of the Apuane Alps and it is composed of three peaks: the *Punta della Croce*, the *Pania Secca* and the *Pizzo delle Saette*.

: Castelnuovo G.: Rocca Ariostesca
  (i.e. Fortress of Ariosto)
: Castelnuovo G.: panoramic view
: The Panie group

VAGLI DI SOTTO

Vagli di Sotto is a sweet little villag[e] enriched by the presence of the 12t[h] century *Church of San Regolo*, domi[nating the large artificial basin i[n] which another small village calle[d] Fabbriche was flooded; when th[e] basin is drained, the hamlet comes t[o] the surface.

1-2: *Vagli di Sotto: the lake*
3: *Campocatino*
4: *Vagli di Sotto: the drained lake with the remains of the old village*

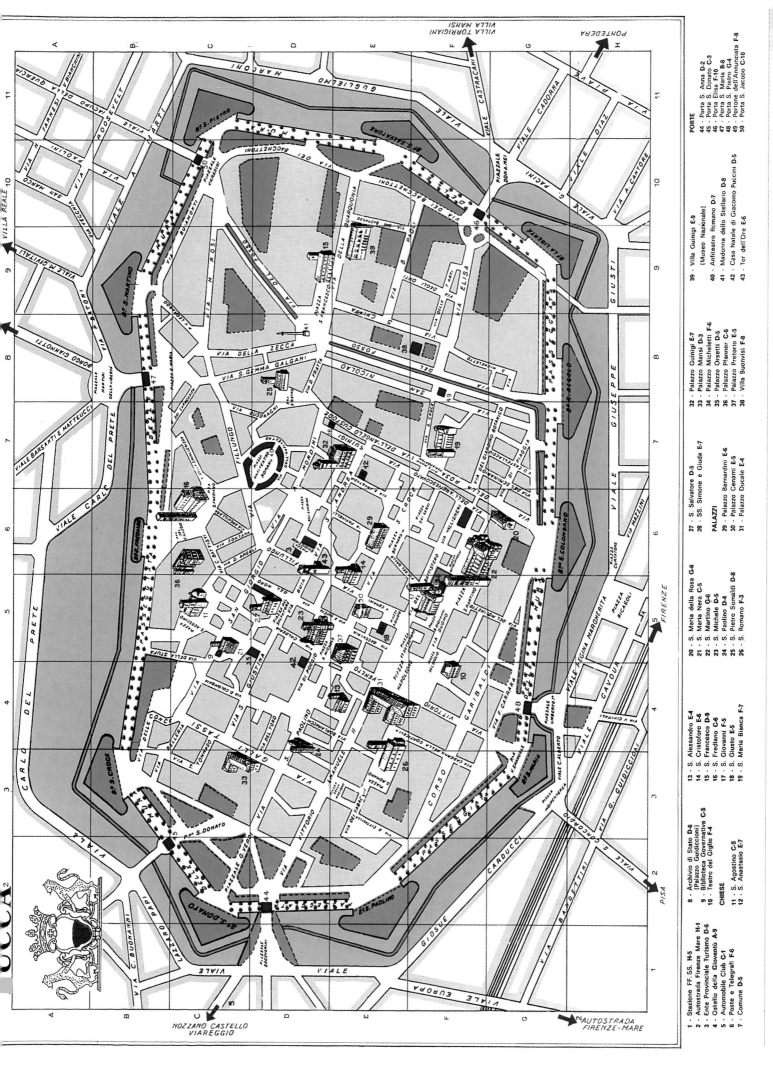

LUCCA

PORTE
44 - Porta S. Anna D-2
45 - Porta S. Donato C-3
46 - Porta Elisa F-10
47 - Porta S. Maria B-8
48 - Porta S. Pietro G-4
49 - Portone dell'Annunziata F-8
50 - Porta S. Jacopo C-10

39 - Villa Guinigi E-9
40 - Anfiteatro Romano D-7
   (Museo Nazionale)
41 - Madonna dello Stellario D-8
42 - Casa Natale di Giacomo Puccini D-5
43 - Tor dell'Ore E-6

32 - Palazzo Guinigi E-7
33 - Palazzo Mansi D-3
34 - Palazzo Micheletti F-6
35 - Palazzo Orsetti D-5
36 - Palazzo Planner C-6
37 - Palazzo Pretorio E-5
38 - Villa Buonvisi F-8

27 - S. Salvatore D-5
28 - SS. Simone e Giuda E-7

PALAZZI
29 - Palazzo Bernardini E-6
30 - Palazzo Cenami E-5
31 - Palazzo Ducale E-4

20 - S. Maria della Rosa G-6
21 - S. Maria Nera C-5
22 - S. Martino G-6
23 - S. Michele D-5
24 - S. Paolino D-4
25 - S. Pietro Somaldi D-8
26 - S. Romano F-3

13 - S. Alessandro E-4
14 - S. Cristoforo E-6
15 - S. Francesco D-9
16 - S. Frediano C-6
17 - S. Giovanni F-5
18 - S. Giusto E-5
19 - S. Maria Bianca F-7

8 - Archivio di Stato D-6
9 - Biblioteca Governativa C-5
   (Palazzo Guidiccioni)
10 - Teatro del Giglio F-4

CHIESE
11 - S. Agostino C-5
12 - S. Anastasio E-7

1 - Stazione FF.SS. H-5
2 - Autostrada Firenze Mare H-1
3 - Ente Provinciale Turismo D-6
4 - Castello della Gioventù A-9
5 - Automobile Club C-1
6 - Poste e Telegrafi F-6
7 - Comune D-5

INDEX

© Copyright 2002 by
Officina Grafica Bolognese
Via del Fonditore, 6/5 - 40138 Bologna - Italia - Tel. 051.53.22.03 - Fax 051.53.21.88
e-mail: ogb@tuttopmi.it

Printed in the UE by Officina Grafica Bolognese   - Bologna - Italy

Layout: Officina Grafica Bolognese

Pictures by: Ascanio Ascani (Misano - FO) - Ghilardi (Lucca) - Maurizio Corti (Lucca)
Carlo Fogliati (Lucca) - Federico Frassinetti (Bologna) - Leonello Mazzotti - Luca Santori (Lucca)